DESERT HARVEST

Rev. Robert A. Wild

LIVING FLAME PRESS

BOX 74 LOCUST VALLEY, N.Y. 11560

Cover: Robert Manning

Published by:
Living Flame Press/Box 74/Locust Valley, NY 11560
ISBN: 0-914544-59-4

Printed in the United States of America.

Dedication

To the Carthusian monks at St. Hugh's Charterhouse, Parkminister, Sussex, England, who were my first guides in the desert.

Introduction

A Trappist monk wrote from New Guinea a few years ago:

> Everyone is called to be a monk today; everyone undergoes the desert experience, like it or not. If anything is needed in this hour, it is men who know their way around in the desert, men who can understand what is going on there, can interpret it, manage with it.

It's always been so: everyone is a monk. Everyone really lives in the desert of his or her own cell, his or her own soul; but today this solitary existence is heightened by the loneliness created by the modern world. Perhaps never before in the history of the world have so many people been forced to live in solitude against their will, forced to enter their personal loneliness because of circumstances. The monk enters these deserts voluntarily, whereas now the world is peopled by reluctant monks who have not chosen to be alone. Their loneliness could become communion. The key, of course, is to _choose the desert_.

For many years I have been blessed with the positive desire to be a monk, to be in the desert. I have chosen to face my personal solitude and aloneness. I have also been blessed, the past 14 years, with a loving community which understands and encourages me in this call.

This book is an attempt to share with all desert dwellers everywhere, the committed and the reluctant, the fruits of what God has taught me. Imagine the power which could be unleashed upon the world if all the barren and fruitless solitudes were transformed into deep communion with God! May these words help to guide all desert dwellers towards this communion.

God Is Our Hope

I have been going slowly, in prayer and reflection, through the prophet Isaiah. The other day I came across this passage which spoke powerfully to me about hope and what hope really is. It's from the 64th chapter: "Oh, that you would tear the heavens open and come down to make your name known, working unexpected miracles such as no one has ever heard of before."

"Unexpected miracles!" In the scriptures, our God is a God who does new and unexpected things. Think for a moment of some wonderful thing, some totally unexpected blessing that happened to you, something you never dreamed would happen, never dared to ask for. In the scriptures, hope is not simply people asking God to help with their own plans. Hope is about *unexpected miracles*.

Think of Joseph, for example, who was thrown into the ditch by his brothers. I'm sure he prayed, "Oh God, get me out of this ditch!" He never would have dreamed of praying, "Oh God, rescue me from this ditch and raise me to a position of great power in Egypt." But that's exactly what happened. God not only rescued him, but because of Joseph's goodness and trust in the Lord, made him one of the great men of neighboring Egypt.

Consider Hannah praying, "Oh God, give me a child." She never would have dreamed of praying, "Oh God, give me a child and let him become one of the great prophets of

9

Israel, so great as to anoint the first king of your people." She never would have asked for that, but that is exactly what happened.

Remember David tending his flock. He probably often asked God for large and healthy flocks when he grew up. He never would have dreamed of asking God to become the chief shepherd of his people, Israel. But that's exactly what happened.

All throughout the scriptures, people have little plans and little ideas. God looks on them and says, "Why are your hopes so small? Don't you know who I am? I am the God who created the universe. I hold the whole future and all possibilities in my hands. You have no idea what I'd like to do for you, what I'm able to do for you, what I desire to do for you."

Even with Our Lady, God was greater than her desires. She was praying for the coming of the Messiah, as all Jewish maidens did at that time. Full of grace though she was, did Mary — even Mary — ever imagine that God himself would come in the flesh? Who did Mary think the Messiah would be? A king greater than David, a prophet greater than Elijah, a priest greater than Aaron, a legislator greater than Moses. But did she ever conceive the plan in the Father's heart? God even said to her, to Mary, "Your plans are too small, your hopes too limited. I myself will come and save my people!"

Who ever would have prayed for that! Who ever would have suspected that God himself would come! Maybe Our Lady's hopes *were* that immense, but certainly no one else's were.

In our own lives we often conceive hope as God helping us out with our small plans. Christian hope is hope in *God*, a God who can do so much more than we could ever hope or imagine. Our God, the God of the scriptures, the Father of Jesus, is Somebody who does totally unexpected miracles. Who ever would have expected the resurrection!

Haven't those of us who have tried to follow Christ in

faith often experienced new and wonderful blessings? Haven't we seen God do things in and around us that have amazed and excited us and filled us with wonder? And he will do much more if we keep following him and put our hope in *him*.

We hope in *God*, not merely in the success of our plans with God's help. *God's plans*, we may be sure, will be much more vast and fruitful than ours. God told Abraham simply to travel west; he told Moses to go to Egypt. He didn't tell them too much else, except that he, the God of gods and the Lord of lords, would be with them.

God is constantly trying to get us to put our hope in *him*. "We don't know what the future holds," it has been said, "but we know who holds the future." So we walk into the future hand in hand with God. It most certainly may not be what we had planned but it will be something much better — what God has planned. Who ever would have expected that God himself would come to save us? What wonders still lie ahead of us in the immense creativity and goodness and omnipotence of God!

Face God

A very brief word that came to me in the poustinia one day was, "Face God."

It is not easy to look steadily into the face of another human being. A really prolonged gaze would require the deepest kind of intimacy, understanding and love. If this is difficult with another human being, how difficult it is to gaze steadily into the face of God.

And yet, this looking steadily into God's face is the most life-giving act of which we are capable. Moses was God's friend and, "The Lord used to speak to Moses face to face, as one man speaks to another" (Ex. 33:11). Moses was a type of all the friends of God and Jesus assures us that we are now his friends. Deep in our hearts we must not be afraid to gaze into God's face.

St. Paul says that now we are all gazing on the glory of the Lord with unveiled faces and being transformed from glory to glory into his very image (2 Cor. 3:18). We become what we contemplate. "Lord of hosts, turn your face towards us and we shall be saved," sings the psalmist. God is always turning his face towards us and he desires that we gaze steadily into his face. Whatever in us shies away from this gaze is not from God. On that day in the poustinia, "facing God" was revealed to me as the source of my true life.

Authentic Experiences of God

Much of scripture concerns people experiencing God. In this meditation, I would like you to reflect on your own experiences of God.

There are many people seeking experiences of God today. We can hardly blame anyone for that. We were made for God; we seek his face everywhere whether we're conscious of doing so or not. Nor can we blame people if they are seeking him in bizarre, or even harmful ways. Most of the time it's ignorance. They don't know where else to look. We must be very compassionate and understanding about people's search for God. Are there any guidelines? Let us look briefly at the scriptures and see what they tell us of God-experiences.

The first wonderful thing we learn is that God certainly *wants* to reveal himself to us and to have us *experience* his presence and his love. The most hopeful part of the scriptural message is that God is seeking his people in order to reveal himself to them. All throughout the scriptures, people are either encountering him, telling about their encounters, running away from encounters, struggling with encounters, or praising God for their encounters with him!

These encounters with God take on a variety of forms.

Sometimes he is recognized as operative in an escape from enemies. Sometimes he meets his chosen ones in lightning and thunder on holy mountains. Sometimes he manifests himself in a physical healing, or in the forgiveness of sins. Sometimes he comes in a gentle breeze. Sometimes he manifests himself by knocking people off their horses in a flash of blinding light. Sometimes people recognize him in an unusual catch of fish. I believe that everyone has had some experience of God at some time in his or her life. The scriptures witness to the many forms this experience can take.

Are there any common features in all these experiences? I believe there are. First of all, most of these experiences of God are unexpected, not planned, not sought after. Samuel was sleeping; Moses was watching his sheep; Peter was fishing; Paul was dashing headlong into Damascus. Most of the time, people are not purposely seeking to experience God. This doesn't mean it's wrong to do so but often in the scriptures God reveals himself to people in the midst of other activities. Besides being unexpected, these experiences are often disruptive of people's lives and plans.

In the cases mentioned above, the experience of God *broke in* on the lives of these men and changed their whole history. Today, with the prominence of process thinking, there is a great deal of emphasis on smooth, natural, step-by-step growth in our awareness of God and his purposes for us. Much of this is true; that's how things naturally grow. But because we are not *in* a natural situation, because we are in a sinful situation, very often God must *break into* our own plans and programs. A tendency today is to fit God and the experience of God into *our* plans instead of the other way around.

This "breaking in" is often, in scripture, an authentic mark of the real God. You may have taken all the aptitude and psychological testings in the world and the overall verdict is that you should be an architect; you may even *want*

13

to be one! God may have other plans. At a certain moment he may break into your life and ask you to be a missionary in Africa!

Or, you may be engaged in following the latest prayer or meditative technique. God may have other plans. He may "break into" your prayer plans and in an instant guide you along another path. It is true that most experiences of the *real* God are of this nature — unplanned, unpredictable, unexpected.

Another characteristic of these biblical experiences is that often they are accompanied, on the part of the person, with feelings of unworthiness, sinfulness, fear, and even dread. There is always the atmosphere of awesomeness when encountering the true God. Even when the experience of being loved by God predominates, as in the baptism of the Holy Spirit, even here the sense of the awesome is not absent.

Too often these days people can be heard speaking of their experiences of God as if they were sucking on some great lollipop. The experiences come across as being all froth and peace and pleasant feelings. One wonders if they're in touch with God or with their own emotional states! The scriptural accounts witness to a profound sense of creaturehood, or unworthiness . . . surrounded by love to be sure . . . but creaturehood and awesomeness nonetheless.

How can we know if we are experiencing God? Look at some of the further criteria.

The experiences of God in scripture *change people's lives.* We cannot really meet God and remain where we are spiritually. Samuel becomes a prophet; Moses becomes the courageous leader of his people; Peter leaves all and follows Christ; Paul changes from a persecutor of Christians to the apostle to the Gentiles. If it is the living *God* we are encountering, we will be challenged to move on from where we are.

God is passionately concerned with the salvation of his

people; his revelation is *salvific*. If he manifests himself to us, it is not simply to have us enjoy his presence. He also says to us, as he said to Isaiah, "Whom will I send?" If we don't hear that dimension of the encounter, we may wonder if we've encountered God.

I'm not necessarily speaking, of course, of a physical sending to go out and accomplish something concrete, though it well may be. But it will most certainly always be a call to move more deeply into God, into love, into the cross, into life. We cannot encounter the living God and remain where we are. "Ho hum, another encounter with God this morning." Was it God or your imagination?

To paraphrase St. Francis De Sales, the goal is not the experience of God but the God of experience. God himself is beyond all the visions of the night, all the flashes of light, all the thunder on the mountain tops. But, Great Teacher that he is, God knows we need experiences to guide us and help us along the way. Little by little, then, he is preparing us for some deeper awareness of him in faith. It will be a constant experience so close to our flesh that it may be years before we recognize he is there. May we have the faith and courage to live in this presence which will be more satisfying than any of the experiences along the way.

Not a Very Nice Idea of Me

When we are at a celebration of the Eucharist and our brothers and sisters are present and there's singing (and probably a number of distractions as well), at such times we ordinarily do not experience any fear of approaching God. At the time for Communion we simply approach and receive into our being the Body and Blood, Soul and Divinity of our Lord Jesus Christ.

But then there are the times we are alone with God. It may be a chapel at night. It's dark. The sanctuary lamp is flickering. When we're alone with God we often ex-

15

perience fear in approaching him.

One of my fears for a long time was that I felt (believed?) that if I ever got too close to God, something really awful was going to happen to me! Isn't that what happened to the saints? If I got too close to God I might break out with the stigmata or I might contract some terrible disease which I will be asked to suffer for the sins of the world.

One night, as I was wallowing in this fear, the Lord said to me, "That's not a very nice idea to have of Me, that your Saviour, your Best Friend, would just be waiting for the opportune time to give you some great suffering."

From that night on I have never been bothered by that thought. It was so clear to me what a truly horrible notion of Jesus that was! Then I thought of the Eucharist.

Every day Jesus demonstrates, in the most direct way his creative love could devise, how close he wants to be to me.

Therefore, when you are alone, when this fear of God comes over you, when you doubt that you are called to anything more than a superficial intimacy with the Lord — and above all, when you have those absurd notions that if you get too close to God he's going to smash you over the head! — when you think like that, remember the Eucharist. Hear Jesus saying, "Take and eat; this is my Body." Trust that word more than all the lying words your mind is conjuring up in the darkness. Realize most of all how those crazy thoughts must hurt the Lord. He loves us so much and we hurt him so much by our lack of trust in his love.

No Famine for Us

"Yes, days are coming, says the Lord God, when I will send famine upon the land; not a famine of bread, or thirst for water, but for hearing the word of the Lord" (Amos 8:11).

16

There is no famine of the Word of God for us. Jesus, our Great God and Saviour, through his wonderful words in the gospels, has laid out for us a magnificent feast and it's ours every day for the eating. Through the mouth of the psalmist Jesus says to us, "Open your mouth wide and I will fill it."

We do not live by bread alone but by every word that comes from God's mouth. For every conceivable question or doubt of the mind, for every desire of the heart, for every dark and lonely and famished place within us, God's Word is present and available for us. All we need to do is open our mouths through faith, chew with desire, then have the courage to swallow God's Word. By faith we recognize it as food; by desire we seek to prepare it for our assimilation; and by swallowing we totally entrust it to our system so that it might give us life.

Are you in doubt about the origins of life and human existence? "In the beginning God created heaven and earth. Let us make man in our image and likeness." Here is the food. Take and eat. Chew and swallow. Allow this truth to dispel the darkness and questionings of your mind.

Do you believe in God but doubt his love for you? "I have loved you with an everlasting love. God so loved the world that he gave his only begotten son." Open your mouth. Eat this word. It is truly health food. Your spirit has been feeding on too much junk food. Eat! Experience the strength of solid, substantial food in your being.

Are you worried about your sins? "Is there no one to condemn you? Neither will I condemn you. Go and sin no more." We can feast on these wonderful words whenever we want to and never get sick, never get fat, never worry about eating too much!

My friend, do you wonder why you don't feel good, why you are sluggish, spiritually overweight? It's because you are eating too much junk food! You are filling your mind with confusion, horror movies, bad news, thousands

17

? me ?

of hours of nonsense on TV, too much laughter, which after a while deadens the simple seriousness of life. The Word of God is true nourishment and it is always available to us. There need be no famine.

Our spiritual systems, like our physical systems, do not need a great deal of food but a modest amount of the right kind. If every day we just fed on a few words of Jesus, chewed them, swallowed them, took them completely into our systems, we would be healthy. If we took just one line — "If anyone loves me, my Father will love him and we will come to him and make our abode with him" — and really allowed this truth to nourish our hearts, it would fill us and satisfy us more than all the other dubious food we feed on.

We tend to make our spiritual diseases such complicated problems and the remedies even more complicated. I think they are not. If we took in the right kind of nourishment every day, spiritually, we would all be a lot healthier. Why do we continue to eat the bread that does not satisfy, drink the water that does not quench our thirst? The gospels are the richest spiritual food the world ever has known, or ever will know. Why do we not feed on it more? There need be no famine for us. "Take and eat," Jesus says to us every day. Yes, take and eat, feed on the Word of God, chew it, swallow it, experience the strength it gives. No one ever need go hungry!

"The Lord Himself Will Set You Free from the Hunter's Snare"

One spring day I was out walking and went to visit a new maple sugar shack we had put up. No one had been in there for several months. It was a very warm, sunny day. Inside, to my surprise, a dozen or so monarch butterflies were flapping frantically at the windows, trying to reach the blue sky outside.

I opened both doors and said to them, "Now's your chance," but they didn't notice the open doors and kept banging away at the windows. So, with my large and gentle hand I approached each one of them, picked them up by the wings and let them out through the doors. As they flew away I experienced something of their tremor of freedom and sense of liberation.

However, two or three would not let themselves be easily caught. As my hand approached, they scooted higher up the window. But finally, they too gave in to my touch and I released them into the sky.

I don't have to spell out in too much detail the lesson the Lord taught me through this little experience. The windows are the mirages of freedom in our lives, false pathways where we flutter around and against which we bang our heads; we call it freedom. We are literally exhausted in our thrashing about. In our deepest heart we suspect that maybe this isn't freedom at all but we keep thrashing anyhow!

Every once in a while the gentle, merciful hand of God approaches. We are threatened by it. We feel this Hand trying to grasp our wings and keep us from being "free." We continue to bang desperately against the windows. We keep eluding this Hand as long as we can.

Then, through some miraculous insight, or perhaps from sheer exhaustion, we pause. We stop struggling. We allow that Hand to grasp our trembling wings. There is a moment of breathless suspense and even a kind of panic. Are we finally headed for destruction?

Suddenly, we experience a release of our powers and the windows are gone. We inhale a wonderful gasp of real fresh air — perhaps for the first time in our lives — and we fly off into the blue sky.

True liberation consists in allowing God to set us free. We fear that his Hand upon us will crush us, will destroy the only freedom we've ever known — this thrashing against the windows of prestige and personality-building and the opinions of others. By allowing him to take us in his Hand, we will find that our freedom is not taken away but released, re-directed. His Hand upon us will guide us to the opening in the sky and we will experience the flight into the true country of our souls.

So, allow God to grasp you in his gentle Hand. It is not death, not a deeper bondage but the beginning of life. It is truly an ending to the mirages of freedom and a launching into unlimited horizons.

Have You Heard the News!

Suppose you turned on the TV set some night and heard, "Ladies and gentlemen, we have wonderful news this evening. A final solution has been found to the arms race, to the world hunger problem, to international crime, ecological concerns, dope, pornography, murder, in fact, all the problems of the world! Isn't that wonderful news?" Without waiting for "the solution," we would think we had tuned in to some movie, or a variety show skit.

If the announcer went on to say, "The final solution to all these problems is the Gospel of Jesus Christ," something in us might be deflated and we might be tempted to think, "Oh, it's just more evangelistic rhetoric about the Gospel."

Our criticism about the latter might not be so harsh but our hearts would have leapt at the mere thought that finally *some* solution had been found to all the evils in the world.

My friends, it's absolutely true. A final solution *has* been found, and it *is* the Gospel of Our Lord Jesus Christ. There *is* absolutely no other solution and the solution of the Gospel *is* absolutely certain.

The world is like a classroom of children who know nothing at all about mathematics and who for a long time have been juggling numbers around without any rhyme or reason. Complete confusion.

Then one day a real mathematics professor comes in and teaches them the simple rudiments of math. He teaches them how to add and subtract and multiply and gives them all the knowledge they require to bring order into their confusion. Then he leaves. Some follow his instructions and continue to bring order into their confused juggling of numbers. Most, however, do not believe the teacher; they continue to scatter numbers around without any order or purpose.

A poor example perhaps but that's what has happened with the coming of the Lord. He has taught the truth about life, how to resolve all our problems and be happy. Most people refuse to follow him; they just continue to create confusion in their lives. They think they are living but they are not. They think they are making history but they are not. The only real history now is doing what the Lord told us to do. The rest is just chaos and confusion. Somehow we should live with that exciting hope which stirred within us when we heard, "A solution has been found to the arms race!" A solution really *has* been found! The dark side is that people refuse to follow the Teacher's advice and so the evil continues. But all the evil in the world should not in the least dampen our joy and enthusiasm that we *know* what the solution is. Isn't that really good news!

Entropy '79

In a magazine article in 1979, I read how professors across the U.S. were characterizing the graduating classes of that year. One comment in particular struck me. A professor said that the students seemed to be without any real altruism, with any causes to challenge their energies and idealism. He said one could almost call the class that year, "Entropy '79." Entropy is a mathematical term for inactivity and the word is sometimes used for the ultimate "running down" of the whole universe — the cessation of all activity.

One of the great sadnesses in the world, which results from a lack of faith in Christ, is the loss of so much youthful idealism, the absence of any cause which would call forth youth's generosity and energies. What a waste especially to see young people without any cause to challenge their energies. Jesus is the answer to this, as he is the answer to everything.

No matter what age we live in, no matter if the environment is being polluted or not, no matter if there's a war or not, no matter if the economy is good or bad, no matter if the whales are in danger or not, no matter what cause may or may not be present, there is always available for everyone the most urgent of all causes, the most sublime of all causes, the most challenging of all causes — spreading the life and light of God become a Man.

Here is the cause of all causes, the challenge of all challenges. It will consume all your energies, all your talents, all your time, all your gifts. It's a cause that will never be out of date, never be fulfilled completely and the more you understand it and live it, the more vast it becomes — the more sublime, the more meaningful. It's a cause as wide as the whole world and more vital and important than all the other causes put together. Its goal is none other than the true healing of the hearts of all the world, the bringing of the Good News of God's love in Jesus.

Oh, no one ever need belong to Entropy '79, or Entropy '85, or Entropy '90, or 2,000! The cause will never be out of date, will never be superseded by any other cause more sublime or more necessary. And the Leader is fantastic! Young people especially need a Leader, a model, a hero; we all do. Our model is Jesus Christ, the greatest Person who ever lived. And he is still alive, communicating to his followers and servants his life and love and strength to continue his mission.

So, graduates of past, present and future, if you're looking for a cause, we offer you the Cause of all causes, the Challenge of all challenges: Help spread the life and love of Jesus Christ. You will never know what idealism is until you stretch the powers of your soul in this cause. The whole world is your arena, all of mankind your goal, with the greatest of all Leaders to lead you! The spreading of the Good News will fill up your tremendous need for an ideal in an exciting way. Class of Entropy '79, unite in the cause of Christ the Lord!

The Two Forces

Since the coming of Christ there are two forces powerfully at work in the world. Every idea, every spirit, every attitude, every movement comes under one of these banners. They are both succinctly stated in the Acts of the Apostles, during the early days of Christian preaching, where these two forces clashed head-on. The first force, the most powerful, the most life-giving, is this: "There is no salvation in anyone else, for there is no other name in the whole world given to men by which we are to be saved." And the second is its opposite: "We gave you strict orders not to preach about that Name."

In some real sense, all the struggles of the world might be explained in terms of these two forces. It may not always be easy to distinguish which movement or spirit or attitude belongs to which force but there are really only these two. The Spirit of Christ says, "Jesus is God. Jesus is alive. Jesus is love. God loves us. Goodness will triumph over evil. Life has meaning. The person is the image of God. We shall live forever. We owe our lives and allegiance to the Lord."

The second force, the anti-Christ (whatever other name or label it might have) says, "Jesus is not divine. Jesus is dead like everybody else. Don't preach in his Name. Life

23

has no meaning anyhow. Evil is greater than goodness. Death is the end of everything. Do whatever you want. There is no God. Why not just admit that and stop all the illusions?" The world is a mixture of these two forces and unfortunately so are the hearts of Christians as well.

The crucial point is that there are really no *neutral* forces. "He who is not with me, is against me and who does not gather with me, scatters." The world has always been filled with a smorgasbord of philosophies and views and ways and approaches to life. I think this is more true today than ever before; also, more than ever before, these views are being broadcast and propagated on a scale hitherto unknown.

So much emphasis today is put on *sincerity*. As long as one is sincere, he or she can be a white witch, an atheist, an abortionist, a revolutionary, a humanist, etc. It really doesn't matter in the long run, as long as one is *sincere*.

God will judge the person; we are not judging persons here. But we certainly can judge ideologies, attitudes, approaches to life. They are either with Christ or against him. They are either *for* his Father, *for* what Jesus preached, *for* who Jesus is, or they are against him. One must choose about Jesus. If you haven't chosen, you are still part of the darkness. We can presume that many of the leaders, scribes, and elders in Acts were sincere but they were forbidding the preaching of the Name, the only Name under heaven by which we can be saved.

Because we don't want to question people's sincerity today, we tolerate all kinds of strange doctrines to float around, believing they are quite harmless. There are no neutral forces now. There are really only two contrary forces: "Jesus is Lord" and "Don't preach in his Name."

What is the alternative?

The Angry Christ

Jesus went into the temple and began driving out those who were selling. . . .

"Oh, no," I can hear the reader say, "not the angry God again! I thought we were just getting over that era!"

Yes, we've all had bad experiences with the anger of God being "mediated" to us through angry authority figures. Yet, for all this, we cannot fashion a Jesus according to our own image and likeness. We must look at the gospels and see them as they really are, see Jesus, as much as we can, as he really is. And, while we must be aware of our wounds of the past in the area of "angry authority figures," we still want to meet *Jesus* and not some figment of our imagination, someone we have fashioned to soothe all our bad memories.

Jesus lives in each of us and this Jesus has great zeal for his Father's house, which each one of us is . . . we are all temples of the Holy Spirit. And, yes, Jesus is infinite love and infinite goodness and infinite mercy *but* Jesus also has great zeal for his Father's house, that is, for each of us.

Perhaps the greater part of this mystery of Jesus cleansing our personal temple must be left to the Spirit's guidance in each of us. So, I put the question to *you*, "Do *you* ever hear Jesus in holy anger saying to you, 'Stop it! That's enough! Stop making my Father's house a den of thieves!' " Do you ever hear a word like that?

You may say, "Well, Jesus doesn't talk like that. Jesus is gentle and kind." But Jesus loves us enough to speak strong words to us. Sometimes he says harsh things at certain times in our lives when we really need to hear a word of reprimand. Jesus isn't just "nice." He is also very jealous about his Father's house.

I think it's part of spiritual maturity to be able to accept the anger of Christ. If we know that he loves us, we will not be disheartened by his anger. His anger is also part of the Good News. He speaks such words to us because he loves us. There are times in our lives when perhaps it is only such a word that will shake us out of our moral slumber. May we not block out such life-giving words when the Lord deems it necessary for us.

Jesus and the Leper

Jesus' encounter with the leper (Matt. 8:2) is such a moving story. "Sir, if you want to, you can cure me." These stories were preserved for us so that we might know what our relationship with the Lord really is. When we come into the Lord's presence, especially in prayer, all kinds of thoughts and emotions go through our minds . . . wonder, hesitation, fear, love. "Is God really listening to what I'm saying? Should I keep asking? Does he care?" These stories in the gospels are given to us to help us understand the answers to these questions.

Imagine yourself as that leper. Imagine what it must have been like to be a leper in the Near East 2,000 years ago, to be someone shunned by all, someone who carried a bell to ring whenever he came close to normal people so they could avoid him. Lepers dressed in rags and people threw rocks at them if their bell-warning didn't come fast enough to suit the "normal ones." They lived in caves and in the holes of the earth.

And we? We don't find it too hard, do we, to identify with some of this. We too often feel we live on the periphery of other people's lives; we all feel in some way that we don't belong. Sometimes we even feel, as we approach others, that we too should ring a little bell of some kind to warn people that we are coming. "Watch out, the leper is coming . . . me!"

One day this man made a decision. For too many years he had suffered from people treating him as the dregs of humanity, so he made a decision, the most important of his life.

"By God, I'm going to do something about this! I don't

care what anybody thinks or what anybody says. They can throw all the rocks they want at me!'' He made a decision to get help, to try to be healed from his leprosy. He had all kinds of human respect and social taboos to overcome but he didn't care; his need was too great.

Who knows the immensity of this man's journey to reach Jesus? Physically, he probably traveled for many miles, pushing through crowds and putting up with the usual abhorrence of people. Spiritually and emotionally, what interior caverns and mountains he had to traverse! All the Gospel tells us is that a leper came to see Jesus but what a struggle, what a journey it must have been!

And then those incredibly humble, pleading, irresistible words of the man, ''Sir, if you want to, you can cure me.'' There's no demand, no self-pity, no arrogance. Just a direct, defenseless, totally disarming request. He lays himself completely before the Lord's mercy. Who could resist such a request? Certainly not God. ''God gives his grace to the humble.''

Jesus stopped. Helping people never ''interrupted'' his schedule! He answered, ''Of course I want to.''

In our prayer relationship with the Lord we project our own small attitudes onto God; we don't adopt the attitudes of Jesus himself. We lepers come to Jesus, dirty and clothed with rags, feeling our isolation and sense of ''not belonging'' to the human race and we say, ''You can heal me if you want to!'' Oh, then we need to hear Jesus' tender words of love to us, ''Of course I want to. This is why I have come. Be cured!''

When this pitiable leper approached Jesus, he did not doubt Jesus' power to heal him but rather, wondered if this Great Man would have any time for him, would think him worthy of attention. After all, there were so many lepers, so many people to attend to.

Maybe when we come before God, that's the concern that is most on our minds. Can Jesus take time for us; are we worth healing? Don't you have to be somebody special for God to concern himself with you? Scripture tells us that

God has no favorites. Positively, that means that each person is a favorite with God. Because of our limitations, *we* must have priorities in our lives, and favorites, I guess. But one of the attributes of God is that he can give his full attention to each person, as if you or I were the only person in existence. Jesus has an infinite amount of time for each one of us. He says to each of us at every moment, "Of course I want to cure you."

"The leprosy left him then and there. 'Not a word to anyone, now,' he said." Jesus didn't always tell people not to broadcast their cures but for some reason he told this man. Jesus wasn't trying to hide the fact that he could heal people. The answer lies in the fact that Jesus deals individually with each person. Perhaps he knew that it would not be good for this man to become the center of attention. Maybe his command had something to do with his own timetable and mission.

When we are healed by the Lord we really need to pray and ask the Lord whether he wants us to reveal the healing or not. Jesus deals individually with *us* as well. Sometimes it may not be his will to speak about our healing. We may be tempted to do it out of pride, or it may fall on deaf ears and cause more harm than good. We need to ask the Lord what he wants us to do. Often we simply dash off like the leper and tell everybody. I don't think the Lord is terribly upset but still, we should pray for discernment about how to handle the healings we receive.

Jesus Continues to Give Scandal

One day, some of Jesus' followers walked away when he told them he was going to give them his flesh to eat. They were scandalized. To scandalize is to scatter stones on somebody's path which can make them trip and stumble. We pray in the psalm, "Lord, make smooth my path."

There are different kinds of scandal. Our sins lead

others into sin. Of this kind Jesus said, "Woe to the world because of scandal." People can be scandalized by our actions because *their* view of reality is too small. In this sense, Jesus scandalized the Pharisees because he healed on the sabbath. Jesus is without sin. We can be sure that whenever his words or anything about his life scandalizes us, it is we who must change.

The Church is the extension, in time, of the risen Christ. Often the very things which scandalized people during Christ's lifetime continue to scandalize people today, when these same actions are done by the Church. We know, of course, that people who make up the Church are sinners and that often their sins scandalize others. It is not this kind of scandal I am speaking about.

Consider the Eucharist. His disciples could not accept the fact that the Lord would (or could?) give them his flesh to eat. Whatever scandalized them about this gift, continues to scandalize people today.

Many are still scandalized with the Catholic Church's teaching that the Eucharist is really, actually, truly the Body and Blood of the Lord. Why this should scandalize people has never been clear to me. Why would people rather have a symbol than the reality? (Interestingly, many of our more fundamentalist brothers and sisters, who take most other parts of scripture very literally, interpret, "This is my Body," symbolically!)

Authority. Many people are scandalized that the Catholic Church teaches and acts in such an authoritative and dogmatic fashion. She does not apologize for such a stance. She is not in doubt about what she believes; she has been precisely commissioned to preserve the true content of the Faith.

It was the same with Jesus. People were scandalized by his authority. "By what authority do you do these things?" One of the diseases of the modern world is scepticism about truth. The Church, like Jesus, does not have an identity crisis. She may be going through upheavals on various levels but she is not in doubt about her faith. Thus, she teaches with authority.

Forgiveness of sins. People are scandalized at the sacrament of reconciliation. Imagine, a priest forgiving sins in the Name of the Lord! Jesus caused a similar scandal. "Who can forgive sins but God alone!" We believe that Jesus passed on this power to his disciples: "Whose sins you shall forgive they are forgiven. . . . " The forgiving priest continues to share in the scandal of the forgiving Lord.

Anointing the Lord's Body. At Bethany, Mary poured very precious ointment over the Lord and thus scandalized some who were present. "This could have been given to the poor." Jesus loved the poor and spent much of his time and effort to relieve their misery; but concern with the poor was not the whole focus of his mission. Just as his own life really centered on his Father's will and pleasure, so too, he intends that a certain amount of our time and effort be devoted to himself alone. "You have the poor always with you but you do not always have me." Thus, his Spirit calls us sometimes simply to sit at his feet and listen to his words; or at another time, to build a beautiful Church to the honor and glory of him and his Father. Some people are scandalized when, in these ways, we continue to anoint his Body and pour out our precious ointments upon him.

There are many things in the Church for which we should blush and which are a scandal to others. We should all pray for their removal but let us not blush or feel guilty or ashamed at those acts of the Church which are the acts of Christ and for which he himself was accused of giving scandal in his own lifetime. Let us rather conform our vision to that of Christ's and never lower his magnificent gifts to our puny level.

The Sacred Triduum
and the Blood of Jesus

For the people of the Bible, blood was *the* symbol of life. "Life is in the blood." The Blood of Jesus, therefore, is *the* symbol of the very life of the Son of God. When he shed every drop of his Blood for us, this was indeed the pouring out of his whole life. I offer you a little meditation on the Blood of Jesus for the Sacred Triduum of Holy Week.

There is no one reaction to blood. It can mean different things, depending on the circumstances.

Once, when out driving, I came across an accident just seconds after it had happened. There was blood all over the highway. It was a horrifying experience.

On another occasion I remember walking for the first time into an auditorium where people were donating their blood. I felt a little queasy, seeing their blood flowing into the containers. But there was something wonderful about all those people taking time out to donate their blood, their life for others.

Another time I had been invited to watch an open heart surgery from a gallery above. I had never seen an operation before and as I watched the surgeons proceed to expose the heart, I fainted!

The Holy Spirit can also inspire in us different reactions to the Blood of Jesus. On Holy Thursday Jesus took a cup and said to his disciples, "This is the new covenant in my Blood." At the sight of this cup being given to them, the apostles, I'm sure, hardly knew what was happening. We, on the other hand, with the knowledge of faith, rejoice exceedingly when, in the person of the priest, Jesus says to us, "Take and drink of this all of you; this is the cup of my Blood. . . . "

On Good Friday the Blood of Jesus was splattered on the ground. Imagine if during a Eucharist somebody came up, grabbed the chalice off the altar and threw the Precious Blood on the floor! How horrified we would be and rightly so. But isn't this, in fact, what a large part of humanity has done through its rejection of Christ . . . thrown his Blood on the ground? At the sight of this Blood staining the earth on Good Friday the Holy Spirit may inspire you to be horrified, or to be sad, or to weep over the spilling of the Blood of the Son of God. Don't resist. Allow your heart to be open to this movement. We *should* be horrified, we *should* weep and be sad over such a sight.

Then, all during Holy Saturday, the Blood of Jesus soaks through the whole earth, right down to the realms of the underworld. Our sadness begins to subside as the earth-tremors quiet down and a holy stillness settles over everything in expectation. We realize that the Blood of Jesus has not been spilled in vain. It is giving birth to a second, new creation.

While it is true that the Blood of Jesus is rejected by many, we also know that his Blood is, for as long as the earth will endure, the most life-giving nutrient of our planet. It is indestructible. No pollution, not even our sins, can ever remove it from our environment. On Holy Saturday we sit in stillness before this Blood as it works its way into the very core of the earth.

Then, Easter morning! The Father says to Jesus (as Jesus said to Lazarus), "Come forth!" As a scientific commentator said about the nature of the image on the Holy Shroud, "The only thing we know that could produce such an image is a blast similar to nuclear energy!" As Jesus explodes from the tomb his Blood becomes radiant from this incredible act of the Father's power.

Now we can look on the shining wounds with great joy and gladness and thanksgiving. His Blood is now and forever the sign of the new life, of the new creation, of his victory. Now begins in our hearts the first chorus of the hymn which shall resound forever: "Worthy are you to receive the scroll and break open its seals, for you were slain. With your blood you purchased for God men of every race and tongue, of every people and nation" (Rev. 5:9).

Scapegoats with Christ

"Denounce him, let us denounce him." "In my anguish I called to the Lord, and he heard my voice." "The Jews fetched stones to throw at Jesus." These are just a few of the many scriptural statements describing the sufferings of the Son of Man. What a mystery! Here we have this most merciful of all persons, a Man who did nothing but heal the sick and speak words of life and love, being attacked verbally and with stones and clubs and finally with hammer and nails.

The image that often comes to me in this context is that of the scapegoat in the Book of Leviticus. On the feast of the Atonement the priest put his hands over a goat and confessed his sins and the sins of all the people. Then the goat was driven into the wilderness, symbolizing a "good riddance" to their sins.

Jesus is our scapegoat. The Father extended his hands over Jesus and laid upon him the sins of us all. In some way the wrath of God, the anger of God, was unleashed upon this meek person, Jesus. Those who have been baptized into Christ share not only in his priestly, prophetic and kingly attributes but we share in this victimhood of Jesus as well, in his being the scapegoat. This is one reason why our sufferings will never be totally understandable to us.

We can pray over each other for healing and that is helpful. We can examine our lives and change and repent of the things causing us or others pain and this is good and essential.

We can attempt to make the structures in which we live more humane and conducive to the Gospel and that will be a step forward. But there will always be a dimension to our sufferings that remains mysterious and not subject to analysis or resolution. This is because we share in the victimhood of Christ. If we can find a reason or a cause for our sufferings, they become easier to bear because somewhat understandable. But then there is the suffering that leads to a self-pity which eats away at us like a cancer.

We must look at Jesus the Scapegoat. Why him? Why all this pain laid upon the Sinless One, the Good One, the Holy One! There are many theories of how the redemption "works" but we don't have to know how it works in order to live by its power and strength. All we need to do is enter into the mystery of Jesus' victimhood, meet him there in faith, unite ourselves with him and we will experience what is perhaps the ultimate resolution of the problem of suffering. It is not a rational, mind-satisfying resolution. It is a resolution of meaning, a conviction that our suffering, joined to that of the Son of God "who loved us and died for us," is ultimately working for our own healing and the good of the world.

Thus, it is not a matter of trying to "figure out" all our sufferings. Some we can; much of it we cannot. It is not necessary to figure it out. It is only necessary to enter in faith into the victimhood of Christ, into the Heart of him who became the Scapegoat for our sins.

"Talitha, Cum"

One of the characteristics of the Gospel accounts of the miracles of Jesus is the absence of anything approaching magical rites. Perhaps the closest we come to anything of the sort (but not really close since the rabbis often did the same) is the instance of Jesus making clay with his spittle and applying it to the man's eyes. This absence of magical rites is very significant, since magicians and sorcerers (witness the Acts of the Apostles) were quite common in the world at that time.

No, what we have is the simple, direct, powerful *word* of Jesus, spoken with assurance and authority. "Only speak the word and my servant will be healed." "I will it, be healed." "Come out of him." "Lazarus, come forth!" The examples are endless and consistent. This directness, power and absolute effectiveness are characteristic of God's Word. When God speaks, it is done. "Let there be light; and there was light."

Not only does God's Word have this absolute power but his Word cannot really be blocked or thwarted. "My word will not return to me void." It may take a long, long time before God's Word succeeds in overcoming the obstacles we put in its way but it is only a matter of time. "Heaven and earth will pass away but my Word will never pass away." And if it never passes away, that means it is always more powerful than the obstacles and that eventually it will accomplish God's intent.

Thus, in the Gospel, we do not really see Jesus "struggling" with sickness, evil spirits, or death. When he wants to, he simply says the word and people are healed, delivered and raised from the dead. The only thing he in any way really must contend with is sin, our freedom, our resistance to his Father's will.

Ultimately, there is no real contest between the Word of God and the various forms of death in the world. "God made everything that it might *live*." God said to every creature, "Live! Be!" This Word is the source of our hope. "The Word of the Lord endures forever." His Word is so powerful that we will always be. We do not even have it in our power to destroy anything. We can change its form, we can retard growth, we can delay life but in, through and underneath everything is the all-powerful Word of God.

A war may kill millions of people; in time, millions more will be born. We can destroy a forest by fire but 100 years later it will be a forest again. We drop bombs on a city but a few decades later the city is rebuilt. Even in the unimaginable instance of nuclear holocaust, it will take the forces of life an unfathomable time to recover. But the recovery will surely happen. Our anti-word, spoken against God's will, is like an interlude, a ripple on the tremendous ocean of life which God has spoken, "Live!"

So, yes, we do have a word. It can be either an anti-word against God's plan, or a word in keeping with that plan. The one is our shame, the other is our glory. We can say to somebody, "You're a stupid fool," and that word can wound and be death dealing. Or, we can say to somebody, "You are a wonderful person," and help bring him to the fullness of life willed for him by God.

I believe that all the evil in the world is due to the anti-words spoken by spirits (demons) and people.

God never said, "Let there be death!" God never said, "Let there be sickness!" God never said, "Let there be sin and hatred and jealousy!" God never said those things, never spoke those words. Rebellious persons have spoken them; and, in comparison with God's Word, they are anti-words, non-words, mistakes. We know God is "in" everything by his immanence; but, if we may express it this way, God is least of all "in" these anti-words. He doesn't want them to be; he doesn't will them and he opposes them with his almighty power!

We cannot be naive about the power these anti-words have. All we need do is look around the world and see their effects, yet in another sense, we believe over-much in their power. There is no contest between our puny anti-words and the Word of God, just as there was no contest between the Word of Jesus and the dark forces in the world of his time.

This is why the "way out" of our evils is to believe in the power of the Word of God. Because sin "clings so close to us," we almost believe that our anti-words and God's Word are equal contenders. It's a great lie. Jesus often could not help people simply because they didn't believe his Word was more powerful than their words of sickness or death. They put their word on a par with his and so remained in their plight.

One of the inspirations of the Spirit I'm most grateful for in the Gospel is the preservation for us, on several occasions, of the actual words of Jesus. We have one instance in

Mark 5:21-43. Jesus was going to heal Jairus' little daughter. "Talitha cum," "Little girl, get up!" Isn't it beautiful to have this powerful Word of Jesus in his own language!

Most of the time, in each of our lives, we have some spiritual or physical disease from which we are suffering. What we need to do is hear, with all the faith we can muster, Jesus saying to us, "Talitha cum!" "Little girl (or little boy) get up! Arise from your selfishness! Arise from your illness! Arise from your unbelief! Arise from your despair! Arise from your fears!" This is the Word of Jesus, God's Word. It is all-powerful, everlasting, never returning to him void. It only "struggles" with the anti-words of death because of our unbelief.

There are two important lines in this story which are most enlightening in connection with the anti-word. People came to Jesus as he was on his way and said to the official, "Your daughter is dead." The next line is very profound and I will give you several translations of it. "Jesus disregarded the report that had been brought"; "Jesus paid no attention to what was said"; "Jesus heard them say this but took no notice"; "Ignoring what they said." And then Jesus said, "Don't be afraid; just believe!"

This line is a profound insight into Jesus' own attitude towards the anti-words of death . . . he disregards them, takes no notice of them. They do not hinder the power of his Word in any way. In short, they really don't exist for him. His Father is not "in" them. He moves against them effortlessly and at will.

The other important phrase occurs when Jesus enters the house and says that the child is asleep, not dead. Again, several translations. "They laughed him to scorn"; "They jeered at him"; "Then they began to laugh in his face."

This is part of our sinfulness and separation from God, the laugh. The laugh of unbelief, the laugh of scorn, the laugh of cynicism, the laugh of sarcasm, the laugh of our own idiocy. "I have been struggling with unbelief, selfishness, jealousy, laziness all my life and you, Jesus, are going to cure me! Don't make me laugh! Don't you see that I'm *dead!* Ha! And you're going to restore me to life!"

Jesus knows full well that we're selfish, lazy, unfaithful, etc. But he disregards, pays no attention to our anti-words. They don't exist for him. He says to us, "Only believe." He says to us, "Talitha, cum! Get up! Come out of your selfishness, arise from your unbelief! Rise from the dead!"

Oh, if only we could really hear him saying those words to us! They are the words of God himself . . . all-powerful, everlasting, not returning to him void. And what a wonderful centering prayer this could be for us, especially in times of need . . . to hear the Word of God, Jesus, speak to the deepest part of our being, "Talitha, cum!" and be free from the laughter of scorn and unbelief!

The Samaritan Was the Neighbor

Whenever we read the beautiful story of the good Samaritan, we are again inspired (hopefully!) to help those in need along the pathways of life. At first glance we take the story to mean that we should assist *anyone* who needs our help, no matter who they are. Who can calculate the number of good deeds which have been inspired by this story of the Lord!

But I have a question for you. Did you ever look closely at the moral *Jesus* drew from his own story? Listen to several translations of his final question to the lawyer. "Which of these three, thinkest thou, was neighbor unto him that fell among the thieves?" "Which of these three proved to be a neighbor to the man who fell into the robber's hands?" "Which of the three do you think was a neighbor to the man . . . ?"

Do you see the mysteriousness of this question? Jesus does not ask, "Which of the three was the most generous and recognized that man in the ditch as his neighbor?" The question is really asked from the point of view of the man who was helped. "As that man was lying in the ditch, who showed himself a neighbor?"

I have deliberately refrained from seeing what the commentaries have to say about this parable (partly because I'm afraid my insight may not stand up under heavy exegesis!), but one day the Lord gave me a slightly different insight into the meaning of this parable. I don't say it's the essence of the story but I think it has something profound to say to us in our daily struggle to love.

What the Lord said to me concerning this parable is that we should *accept* help from anybody. If the man in the ditch hadn't been so beat up, would he have accepted help from the Samaritan?

Love has to do not only with actively helping, loving others but in allowing ourselves to *be* loved, to *be* helped by others. Which do you think is harder? They're both hard but I don't think we can reach the purity of heart in loving others unless it more and more flows from a heart which is open to being loved as well.

Many people are very intent on watching for the beaten person along the road so they can help him. This is wonderful. But are we equally aware that, for others, *we* are the person along the road and they are seeking to help *us?* This parable is addressed not only to those who refuse help to others; it is also addressed to those who refuse to *be* helped.

Isn't it true that we are very selective in accepting help? How often we refuse help from a certain person because we don't like him or her, or because we don't want to get involved, or because we're afraid he or she may then expect us to help *them!* In other words, allowing ourselves to be helped is another way of creating relationships.

"Go and do likewise." Go and do what? Go and allow Samaritans to help you. That's often harder than using all my wealth and strength to help poor so and so out of the ditch. Sometimes the poor so and so is me!

Tear Open My Heart and Come Through!

St. Paul tells us in so many, many ways that we have been joined to Christ. So often Paul talks about our being *in* Christ, our being *with* him and that our deepest life is hidden *with Christ* in God. St. Peter says that we have become sharers of the divine nature. Our true life is the life of Christ in us. We will never completely understand that, here or in eternity. It means that the Christian life is not simply our own life plus a "life of Jesus" which aids us, changes our thoughts and attitudes a little bit and helps us to "get through life." No. Our *life* is Christ; our real life *is* Christ.

The Christian life . . . and the chief work of the Holy Spirit . . . has everything to do with becoming aware of this life of Christ more than our own life. Hence, the mystery of Advent has to do with allowing ourselves to experience the desires of *Christ himself;* it is not first and foremost a preoccupation with our own desires. Yes, desire Christ to come. But what is in us (because Christ is in us) is the *very longing of Christ himself to come.*

During Advent we celebrate three comings . . . the Incarnation, Christ's coming at every moment and his final coming. Imagine God looking at the world 2,000 years ago. What a longing he must have had to come and save us! We share in that, or rather, that very desire of Christ's is in us through his presence. And imagine Jesus' desire to come at the end of time to claim his kingdom and hand it over to the Father. Yes, we long for the kingdom to come. But what must Jesus' longing be for the kingdom of his Father to finally come! This desire of Christ is in us because *he* is in us.

So that's the first thing we should do, join our desires to those of Christ's. But what else can we do? All during Advent we're going to sing "O Come, O Come, Emmanuel!" Besides desiring his coming, we also have within us the power to *effect* his coming into the world.

40

The first word of Jesus in Mark's gospel is "Repent!" This presupposes true freedom on our part; we must have some real power to be able to do that. "Behold I stand at the door and knock. If any man open I will come in. . . . " This means we ourselves have the power to open. It means we have the power to allow him an opening through which to manifest more fully his presence in the world. There is, then, the immensity of God's desires to come and there is our freedom to allow him to come. Then why doesn't he come?

He doesn't come as completely as he would like because he's blocked by our freedom. Human hearts are the windows, the doors, through which God's presence comes. He can't come fully because we hold the keys to these entrances and we will not open to him. Our prayer cannot simply be, "O God, tear open the heavens and come down!" He has *already* torn open the heavens. What he is powerless to tear open is our hearts. What we should be praying is, "Tear open my heart and come through!"

How much do we really want God to come into the world? We pray for an end of the arms race and that is good. But do we pray for an end of the wars in our hearts? Do we pray . . . and take some practical steps . . . to end the fighting between myself and the people with whom I live, or work, or who live down the street? Do I want God to come into the world enough to really desire him to come first into the warring in my own heart? Yes, rend the heavens and come down but most of all, "tear apart my own heart and come through me!"

Our own heart is the only reality in the whole universe we really have any freedom over. We can give talks and write books. We can pray that other people change. We can demonstrate to express our views. We can write letters to leaders . . . all good things. But the effectiveness of such actions is really out of our control. What is in our power absolutely and what is absolutely sure of hastening the coming of God, is the opening of our own hearts.

The saints understood this very well. I suppose they too tried for a while to change others, or structures. Eventually they understood that if God was ever to do anything concretely, they would have to let him do it through them. From thence forward they stopped trying to change others and put all the emphasis on themselves. They said to God, "Come through me into your world and I don't care what it costs." God did and that's why their lives are the real history of the world, because it's the history of the eruption of the kingdom into the world. All other eruptions simply compound the problems.

This is really the challenge of Advent. God came into the world at Christmas. But why did he come? So that he could win over our hearts and come into them as he came into Mary's. Yes, we also long for the final coming of Christ at the end of time. But if we don't allow him to come now, we're going to tremble at his final coming. Jesus has already come in the flesh; I don't know how or when he's going to come in judgment at the end of time. All I know is that *now* he longs to come into our own hearts, to complete the work of his Incarnation and to obviate his need to come to us in judgment at the end. He would rather come now in mercy and gather us into the kingdom of his Father.

"Oh, Jesus, yes, come and destroy the idols in the world which people worship instead of you . . . power, pleasure, money, ambition. But destroy them first in my own heart. Demolish them despite my reluctance and halfheartedness. Yes, come and dispel the darkness of ignorance in the world but shatter it first of all in my own heart. Cure me of my warped love for the darkness and my fear of the light. Humble the pride of the world which seeks to find life without you; but, oh, first, Lord, humble my own heart. Humble me most of all, before anyone else. Yes, manifest yourself to the world which needs you so much. I want this so badly that I give you full sway, first of all, to manifest yourself through me."

The one who fulfilled all this best was Our Lady. I don't

42

believe that she considered herself worthy to be the Mother of the Messiah. I believe, though, that her desire was so intense for the coming of the Messiah and so pure, so total, that she made of herself a perfect opening for the Father. Then since she was blinded by her own humility, she became the chosen vessel. See what happens when one heart is totally open to the Lord's coming!

In the Gospel, Jesus said that if anybody does the will of his Father, that person becomes his brother and sister and mother. We have it in our power to become the mothers of Christ, to give him birth in our time and place. In some astounding way we have the power to *make* him come into our world. He wants to come. We have the key . . . our freedom, our generosity, our love. "Yes, Lord, come to the leaders of the world, the Church, to those who are able to effect loving and just changes. But mostly, come through me!"

Dealing in Faith with Bad News

The ever-present nuclear arms madness, past events such as the Cuban missile crisis and the Falklands confrontation, and the daily anxiety that something accidental may happen to the computers controlling the weaponry . . . these and many mini-crises pose a serious question to the Christian. "How does one relate in faith to all this?" I'm not thinking here so much of political activity in the ordinary sense, although I consider what I'm about to say as concern and "action" for the body politic in the deepest sense of those words.

These "wars and rumors of wars" create anxiety and, if we are not watchful, can increase darkness, hopelessness and confusion in our own hearts . . . the very things which are causing the wars. Our very first call from God, then, is to be watchful over our own hearts, that part of the world over which *alone* we have any direct control.

The first and very best thing we can do, whether in times of crisis or not, is to deepen our faith in the resurrection, to live as "children of the resurrection." No matter what is happening in the world, Christ is risen from the dead. No matter what crisis is going on, Jesus is alive and he will never die again. Nothing that is happening, or that ever will happen, can change that fundamental deed of the Father. Whatever wars are going on, whatever conflicts may come, Christ is risen from the dead and he always will be risen.

This is not only the central truth of all of history, it's the only source of life for the world. To allow anything to dim that truth in our hearts is the greatest of all tragedies for the world, a greater tragedy even than another war.

Whatever is happening in the world, witness to the resurrection! Nothing can alter that truth. We have to guard our minds and hearts so that the bad news doesn't weaken our faith in the resurrection. That would be the worst news of all . . . really bad news. We can be sad and concerned about the world, as we should be. But it's crucial that our own hearts do not participate in the darkness by a weakening faith in the resurrection.

The second thing we can do when we hear about crisis is to pray more. As Christians, we do not believe prayer is escapism, or a way of salving our consciences, or "all we can do anyhow." For us, prayer is a real force in the world. And we probably shouldn't pray generally — "that communism be stopped," or "that the arms race would cease." "Communism" and "arms race" don't exist. We should pray specifically for individual people's hearts to be converted . . . the rulers of nations by name, or those who are heads of defense departments, or any other individuals whom we know can effect a real change. It is *people* who make decisions and so it is people who need to be enlightened and converted.

Thirdly, the very best thing we can do for the world and for our own wholeness and sanity during times of crisis, is to continue to do what the Lord is asking of us — in our homes, businesses, or wherever we happen to be. What good does it do to mope around, thinking of the problems of the world!

There is a small but important part of the world that has been entrusted to our care. It may not be the whole of America, or the entire province of Ontario but it is something concrete and definite, something worthwhile and important. And what is more, it is something actual and within our abilities and competence. To wish we were elsewhere, or to believe that if we *were* elsewhere, we certainly could effect a change in the critical situation, is pure illusion! The best thing you can do for the world in times of crisis is to care for that part of the world the Lord has entrusted to you. If everyone did that, there would be no crisis at all!

These three approaches, then, I believe, are the first steps Christians need to take before they think of doing anything else. Don't allow anything to weaken your faith; pray for those who are in positions to effect a change; continue to do peacefully what the Lord is asking of you. If all Christians did these things during crisis and did not dissipate their energies through lack of faith, failure to pray and neglect of their duties, the world would continue to be transformed into the kingdom, despite what the children of this world were doing.

Kissing the Land

Long before the 4th of July was the national holiday for America, it was the feast of St. Elizabeth of Portugal. She was a Queen and a Saint; that is, she had wonderfully reconciled in her own heart the relationship between her country and the Gospel of Our Lord Jesus Christ. On such days as the 4th of July, or whatever might be your own country's national day of pride, we too struggle to see our countries in the proper light of the Gospel. On such days, I offer you, for your meditation, a powerful symbol. It's a symbol we've all seen. And I will not so much try to explain it as invite you to enter into it so that the Lord himself can instruct you. The symbol I offer you is that of our Holy Father John Paul II, kissing the soil of each country as his first gesture when he gets off the plane.

Pope John Paul has kissed the soil of Nicaragua, Haiti, Mexico, Guatamala, England, the United States, Poland, France and if he ever goes to the Soviet Union, he will kiss its soil as well.

What is he kissing? He is not kissing the military regimes. He is not kissing the presidents of the countries. He is not kissing their laws and constitutions. He is not kissing democracy or socialism or communism or dictatorships. He is kissing the land, the nation, the magnificent march and movement of a people throughout their history to discover freedom and happiness and their destinies.

He is kissing the soil which has grown their food, soaked up the blood of their wars, the soil on which their homes are built and in which their dead are buried. He is kissing the soil saturated with the sweat from their labor, the tears from their joys and sorrows, the wine and beer of their rejoicing. This is why he said, when asked once why he kissed the ground, "The earth is sacred. It is our mother, our homeland."

It is fashionable today to be "citizens of the world," to do away with all national loyalties. I think this is not always free from illusion; I think it often disregards the proper love of one's country which is perfectly compatible with the Gospel. It's part of the gift of piety to have a love for our origins, for everything and everyone who has helped us become what we are. In our younger years we feel the need to "split off" from parents, country, so as to "become our own person." That's okay; it's normal. But part of maturing is to gradually reappropriate and reintegrate in ourselves all the benefits we have received from parents and country . . . to be grateful for them and appreciative of them.

Our national holidays are days for kissing the earth. It may not be a bad thing for you yourself to do on that day. You're not kissing the present government. You're kissing the land and the people which have been your place in the universe to grow and seek your destiny. Such a place is to be reverenced and loved!

It Was Me!

There is an Eastern rite prayer we pray at Lauds every morning during Lent. "Lead me on the path of salvation, O Mother of God, for I have profaned my soul with shameful sins and have wasted my life in laziness. When I think of the many evil things I have done, wretch that I am, I tremble at the fearful day of judgment."

One of the spiritual sensitivities, one of the spiritual longings that goes through me every time I recite that prayer is that I hope to God that someday . . . someday . . . I will really be able to take responsibility for my sins without blaming anybody else or anything else. "Yes, I've sinned, but look at the upbringing I've received! Yes, I've sinned, but how could I do otherwise considering the circumstances? Yes, I've sinned, but I am subject to so many unconscious forces."

I think one of the deepest longings in all of us is that some day, we will be able to say to God in all honesty and truth, "It was *me*. I did it. I'm responsible. I'm a sinner. Lord, have mercy." Oh, what a breath of fresh air that would be to our souls! What a burden it would lift from our hearts!

Is there a way to have this sentiment become a reality? There is. Admit to yourself that there is something *right now* in your life that is sinful and for which you are totally responsible. Just the thought of it scares us, doesn't it? But it's true for each of us. At this moment there is something sinful in my life.

We probably don't have the spiritual and psychic energy to face that every day. We're supposed to admit this at the beginning of the liturgy but often it doesn't go very deep. That's why the Church has special seasons of penitance, like Lent and Advent. They are times to allow this truth to enter into us as deeply as possible.

This moment can also be today . . . now. We can ask the Holy Spirit to reveal to us a sinful area of our life. We can allow that healing truth to transform our hearts and then with courage and honesty we can say, *"I am a sinner."*

The fathers of the desert called this true knowledge. Once it is known and accepted in the heart, many other aspects of life fall into place. We begin to accept sufferings of whatever kind as just punishment for our sins. The wounds of Christ become more precious to us, admitting now that they were for *me* and not first of all for "those others." There is a way, in the Spirit, of accepting our sinfulness that is not morbid, not depressing, not spiritually masochistic. That we are sinners is simply the truth. It is a wonderful grace, greatly to be desired, to know this truth in a life-giving way.

Wrong for So Long

There are many obstacles to conversion. One of them is admitting that we may have been sinning, or doing something stupid, for a long, long time. That is a very hard pill to swallow. We put up a tremendous number of defenses around defects and sins that have been with us for a long time. It's extremely difficult to admit that we've been wrong for so long!

One day I was spinning wool in the poustinia. After you get two balls of single yarn you then ply them together to make the two-ply yarn. Well, I was happily plying away but things weren't going too smoothly. No matter. Perhaps the wheel needed oil or something. I barged ahead.

But the spinning kept getting tougher and tougher. Having almost completed the whole ball, I suddenly realized that I had plied *in reverse!* Then I had an experience, the kind I'm trying to convey. You reach a moment of "enlightenment" when you realize that you've been doing it all wrong, all the time! Not only that but now to "get it right" you must go through a whole long and messy process.

In the case of the wool, it went something like this. The whole ball had to be unravelled! The initial realization was very painful; I could hardly get up the energy to begin. But once the truth of my stupidity was accepted, it got easier and easier. There was spun wool all over the poustinia — the rafters, the floor. It looked like a huge spider web! As I approached the final rewinding, there was a great sense of joy and gratitude.

We have not been perpetrating all of our sins and stupidities for many, many years, only some of them. We need a great deal of humility to face the truth that we may have been involved in some wrong-doing or stupidity for so long. Perhaps the older we get, the harder this is to face. We may get glimmers that something is wrong but we quickly push it out of awareness. A sin or mistake lasting ten years of our life is just too hard to take.

If we allow this awareness into our hearts, be sure that our first reaction will be filled with pain, frustration, a sense of hopelessness . . . as with my spinning. Our first reaction will be a cry, "Oh no! You mean I've been wrong all these years?"

Yes, it may have been all wrong for a long time. Just being able to say this, though, is a great grace from God. Our long-standing defects are the hardest to uncover and to repent of. There will be a tendency to deny it, to make believe it's not as bad as you think. It probably *is* as bad as you think! Accept it. Don't rationalize your way out of it.

Believe me, it's a great grace!

Discouragement can set in! "If I've been wrong in this area, maybe my whole life is one big mistake." Sadness . . . "All my efforts have been wasted. There's no sense in trying any more." Self-pity . . . "I'll never be able to live right."

This is an important moment of decision. We're either going to admit our blindness and seek change, or we're going to cover it up and continue on as if nothing has been revealed to us.

It was very, very difficult to start unravelling that dumb yarn. "All that time wasted!" But as I proceeded, joy was restored. After all, we can't deny reality like that. If we break something, we have to pick up the pieces. If we make a mistake, we admit it. And, if we discover that we've been sinful or immature or childish in some area of our life for a long, long time, the really mature and realistic and life-giving thing to do is *admit it* and unravel, as best you can, the mistake.

Repentance, after all, is admitting that we have been traveling down the wrong road and the longer we have been traveling down that road, the harder to admit our mistake. (Like when we're out driving and we discover that we've gone 200 miles in the wrong direction!)

It takes a big heart to repent. "Why didn't God reveal this to me sooner? Why did he let me waste so many years of my life?" It won't help at all to think like that. Probably God tried to reveal this sin to us many times in the past but we didn't have the courage to face it. I'm sure it wasn't God's fault!

Facing long-standing faults is a great grace, the stuff that saints are made of. You will know both the pain of having wasted many years and the joy of finally living in the light. So start unravelling the yarn!

"I Didn't Tell You to Do That!"

I think it was Watchman Nee who, in one of his books, related how he tried to do something for the Lord and it turned out disastrously. He asked the Lord why, and he heard the Lord say to him, *"I* didn't tell you to do that!"

While I'm sure many contemporary Christians have heard of Watchman Nee, I'll wager not many have heard of Isaac of Syria. Isaac of Syria is a profound spiritual guide who lived at the end of the sixth century. You can find a spiritual gold mine of his wisdom in *Early Fathers From the Philokalia.* I highly recommend him.

It is extremely important to remember that two thousand years of Christian life have gone before us. Our brothers and sisters down through the ages were very close to God and God taught them deep spiritual truths and wisdom. I doubt that we can learn anything really too new about our life with God which the Spirit hasn't already taught somebody, some place, at some former time. If we were more in touch with the great treasures of our heritage, we would have access to much more wisdom.

Take this matter of wondering why some of our "good" inspirations don't turn out so well, as in Nee's case. Isaac of Syria knew all about the truth that some of our "good" inspirations don't always come from the Holy Spirit. He has a short passage where he lists half a dozen reasons why a "good" inspiration may *not* be from God. When we start out in our life with God, we're busy sorting out the good from the bad. As we progress, we need more and more to sort out the apparent good from the really good.

Isaac writes: "Sometimes a man desires something good but God does not help him. This happens because at times a similar desire comes from the devil and is harmful instead of useful. The devil uses all his wiles to offer this activity in a favorable light, [so as] to incite us to it and thus disturb our peace of soul or cause harm to the body. So we must carefully examine even our good desires."

St. Isaac then goes on to list reasons why a certain good may not be from God.

We believe in evil spirits and know that some of our "good intentions" may come from them. But we believe these "good" intentions can also proceed from sinful areas within ourselves. As we read some of the discernments of St. Isaac, we will discover that "good inspirations" may come not only from evil spirits but from our pride and/or ignorance as well.

"What we wish is beyond our powers."

Some of our "good" inspirations prompt us to achieve things which are really beyond our present physical and/or spiritual capacities. This is rocky terrain. We know and believe that God can and often does call us to difficult things — to step out in faith, to reach beyond where we are, to walk the extra mile. The Gospel constantly calls us to stretch our spiritual capacities.

At the same time, there is a pride in us that tends to blow up our actual capacities out of all proportion to our abilities. Thus, people attempt penances that ruin their health, or choose certain very difficult apostolates which then lead them to discouragement. The lives of the desert fathers are filled with examples of such misjudgments. The devil does not care *how* he stops us, whether by committing actual sin or by pushing us beyond our capacities, thus leading us into discouragement and frustration. As long as he *stops us*, he uses either good or bad means.

"Or because it is alien to the form of endeavour we have accepted."

There are many "good" inspirations that do not fit in with our present vocation and which become a source of unpeace for us. We are married and feel called to be a missionary. We are a contemplative religious and feel called to the market place. We are a missionary and feel called to become a Trappist. We are doing good work in our parish and feel called to start a prayer group outside the parish. The examples are endless.

Again, this is delicate terrain. Some of these movements *can* be from the Holy Spirit but my guess is that a high percentage of them are not. They often proceed from our restlessness, from our failures to come to grips with all the potentialities in our present life situation. We all believe that the Holy Spirit is pushing us to grow but most of the time it is to be presumed that the pushing from God will be right within our present vocations.

"Is the inspiration in keeping with our basic life vocation and situation?" That is the vital question.

"Has the time come for this inspiration to be fulfilled or begin to be fulfilled?"

Some good inspirations may be from the Lord but not for *now*, not for *this moment*, or *this day*, or *this month*. Some inspirations are the beginnings of dreams that the Lord wishes us to tuck away in some place in our hearts until, in his own good time, he opens the doors and brings those dreams to fruition.

Many inspirations of the Lord are life-seeds. He plants them, but it is not possible (nor does he desire) that we gather the fruit *tomorrow*. Our impatience can seek to ripen these inspirations prematurely.

Jesus could only do what was pleasing to the Father, only say what the Father taught him to say (John 8:28-29). A certain number of our "good" inspirations are not from the Father but from our pride, or our ignorance, or from evil spirits. May the Spirit of Jesus enable us to discern which is which!

I Don't Want to Play!

They are like children squatting in the town squares, calling to their playmates, "We piped a tune but you did not dance! We sang you a dirge but you did not wail!"

For years this remark of Jesus was an enigma to me. (It has been a long time since I was a child!) Then one summer, not too long ago, I was watching a group of children trying to organize a game. One little boy was asked if he wanted to play baseball. He said no, he didn't like baseball; he liked kick ball. The other children quickly agreed, "OK, let's play kick ball!" The boy thought for a moment, then walked away saying, "No, I don't want to." Apparently, it wasn't either baseball *or* kick ball that was the issue; something else was bothering him. Jesus must have observed similar scenes sometimes in Nazareth, sitting in front of his carpenter's shop and watching the children on the street.

We are often like this in our relationship with God. We make a pretense at wanting to know God's will but when he shows us something he would like us to do, we often say, "No, Lord, I don't want to do *that*" (implying that if it had been something else, we would have responded immediately). Yet if God invites us to that something else, we, like little children, again say, "No, I don't want to do that either." We actually believe (in a childish way) that we are simply not being presented with the right option. In reality, we don't want to do *anything*.

The Pharisees used this same kind of thinking when they proposed that they were eagerly seeking the Messiah. "It couldn't be John . . . fasting like that and living like a wild man. He was insane! It couldn't be Jesus either. Look how he eats and drinks! Would the Messiah act like that?"

Jesus read their hearts. They didn't want to play at all; they weren't open to any kind of grace. Sometimes in our life with the Lord, we act like that. We kid ourselves by saying that God is just not approaching us in the right way. If he did, we certainly would play. But isn't it true that often we don't want to play at all . . . neither dance or sing a dirge? The problem is much deeper.

Christian Self-Denial

Jesus is *for* life, immense, unending, exuberant life. He is not only *for* life. Whatever life *is,* that is what *he* is. "I *am* the life." Jesus is not against sex or the body or money or clothes or food. The only thing he is really against is sin, that which runs counter to his Father's will.

Today there is a great deal of emphasis on the goodness of everything. It is almost becoming a heretical idea that one should in any way "deny oneself" any of these good things. Self-denial is labeled (in slick psychological terms) as sadism or masochism or (in slick philosophical terms) as Manicheism or Stoicism. No doubt, the aberrations designated by these labels may be partially at work in some Christians' efforts at self-denial. Our hearts are not perfect; our motivations are not all pure. But a danger greater than all the aberrations is the misguided attempt to do away with self-denial altogether. What shall we call *this* heresy? I can't think of one word but it would be a Christianity which practically denied original sin, the fact that our hearts are infected with sinful attitudes. Creation is all right. It's *my heart* that's the problem.

St. Paul says that we have been entrusted with the mysteries of God . . . to know and understand them ourselves and to be able to communicate them to others. One of the greatest mysteries with which we have been entrusted is the mystery of life through death.

In the Gospel we read statements like, "Deny yourself and take up your cross every day and follow me"; "If your hand scandalizes you, cut it off"; "Unless you hate your father or mother, you cannot be my disciple." These commands can be and have been misunderstood, both by Christians and non-Christians alike. You can read histories of monasticism written even by Christians who view monasticism pretty much as a misapplication and misunderstanding of the Gospel. People opposed to Christ write off the Gospel as contrary to life and enjoyment labeling it a world-denying, creation-denying doctrine. It is not true. Jesus' words are spirit and life. All other words in the world, which try to say what life is, will pass away but Jesus' words will never pass away.

I take it, therefore, as a truth of the Gospel, that we must deny the self, but how, and why? I will use fasting as an example — but only as an example — for I believe the interior motivation I'm trying to describe applies to other forms of self-denial as well. Also, I believe there is in the human heart an instinct to deny the self, an instinct which takes on many different forms and expressions. The Spirit of Jesus alone can reveal to us the true nature and meaning of this instinct.

Consider, then, the matter of food. Food is good; yet we all know we must put a curb on our eating. We must limit both the amount and kind lest we damage our system. Here already we have the principle that some kind of limitation is necessary. It is a rational, secular, merely human motive, but part of God's order. Many people — everyone — "fasts" like this, but it is not Christian fasting. If you fast in a Christian sense, it will *also* have beneficial physical effects but Christian self-denial is not primarily motivated by health reasons.

Sometimes we fast, or live more simply, in order to identify with other people in the world who are hungry, or who lack the necessities of life. This is laudable but not necessarily Christian. There are many people today who, out of a sense of justice or sympathy, try to identify in some concrete ways with their suffering brothers and sisters. If you fast or do penance, this can *also* be one of your motives but it is not yet the depth of Christian asceticism.

Another motive (which at first may *seem* to be at the heart of Christian asceticism and, indeed, is close to it) is that by fasting I will get closer to God. In a religious sense, this is the reason, of course, why people fast and do penance. The Christian *will* get closer to God by fasting if the interior attitudes and dispositions of the Spirit are present. There is no *necessary connection* between not eating and getting closer to God. (In this context I often think of all the wasted dieting and weight-watching that goes on these days. If only such discipline could be invested with motives that would bring people closer to God as well as closer to their desired weight!)

Well, what are these attitudes and dispositions of the Spirit that make acts of self-denial really life-giving and Christian?

Any act of self-denial only has real value to the extent that it partakes of the Lord's own passover from death to life. Our little acts of self-denial only receive value because of Christ's passage from death to life. Jesus took on and sanctified the whole mystery of death, not simply little acts of dying. It is by entering interiorly into this total sweep of his victory that our self-denial achieves its ultimate value and effects within us its complete saving action.

What does this mean exactly? The physical difficulty of self-denial is not the hardest part. Movie stars, athletes, and others, can fast tremendously and within a few weeks lose a great deal of weight. It is possible to simply lose weight without being open to the mystery of death itself, possible to suffer physically in many ways without allowing that suffering to be joined to Christ's passover into life through faith in him. One can be losing weight physically and still be unloving, distracted from God and compensating on many other levels for the absence caused by this denial of food.

Here is the main point: every form of suffering, whether it is voluntary or involuntary, carries within it a rumbling of death, final death, the mystery of death itself. Christian asceticism is consciously and willingly entering with Christ into the total mystery of death on all possible levels. Whether the penance or self-denial is fasting or silence or disciplined reading, the ultimate goal is not simply the raising of consciousness, or better health, or even identification with the less fortunate. The ultimate goal is to allow this penance to sweep us into Christ's passage out of all deaths into the life of the Father.

This essential component of Christian asceticism is a definite act, an interior disposition, a grace of the Spirit. It is a willingness to pass with Christ through death itself. It is this grace which both gives ultimate value to Christian asceticism and which also makes self-denial *really hard.* It makes it hard because you must face death itself, not merely some little physical death. In this sense, it is harder to fast with the proper dispositions of faith than merely to give up a great quantity of food in order to feel or look better. The "hardness" comes in the interior disposition.

On the other hand, once the grace of the Spirit takes hold of us in a deep way, this disposition is most powerful for sustaining people in practices of self-denial in a meaningful and life-giving way. Witness the deeds of the saints. At a certain point they see, with their interior eyes, that this dying in Christ is the true way to life. It is not masochism, not stoicism. The real secret of life has been revealed to them: life through death.

Isn't it true that the real pain of pain is that it reminds us of death? Who of us can really be sick in any serious way and not think of death itself? Isn't it true that, if we allow ourselves to reflect, there is in every pain this rumbling of death itself, the mystery of death? Christian asceticism is the conscious entrance into this mystery.

The truth is that we are tending towards death day after day. Jesus calls us to "practice dying." (Someone asked a young boy dying of cancer if he was afraid. "Yes," he said, "I've never died before.")

Jesus calls us consciously to practice dying. You will experience that this dying, if it is done with the right dispositions, adds a tremendous zest to life. The fear of dying keeps robbing our joys of their depth dimension. All our joys are truncated because we know they will end. Our facing of death in true asceticism will increase our awareness that joy will continue forever. Paradoxically, facing the death dimension in earthly things increases our satisfaction in them when we use them. We can experience the joys more completely because we've accepted in some absolute way the fact of their limitations.

The key to Christian self-denial is really to enter whole-heartedly into the mystery of Christ's ultimate passover, to enter it in the depths of our hearts. It is a kind of absolute stepping off of the earth and that is what frightens us. Jesus said an absolute yes to every pain, an absolute yes to death itself. Our asceticism must include this same comprehensive yes. Those people who have had "life after life experiences," who have been medically dead and then come back — live life with a new zest because they have said yes to death, are no longer living with emergency brakes on, no longer avoiding the thought of death. Rather they are now drawing life from it.

Thus, if every day, through true Christian asceticism, we can practice dying with Christ, immerse ourselves interiorly in the full sweep of his passover to the Father, we will possess and be living one of the great secrets of life . . . perhaps the greatest: how to live joyfully and with zest in the face of the rumblings of death all around us.

The Beautiful Pink Mist

Ten years after his release from prison, Solzhenitsyn wrote, ''The archipelago was lost in a beautiful pink mist of rehabilitation, and became altogether invisible. . . . But I (even I!) succumbed. . . .' As the paunch grows, the memory goes. I did get fatter. I fell for it and . . . believed . . . believed what my own new-found prosperity would have me believe. I let myself be persuaded by the complacent mainland. No, we are creatures of mortal clay! Subject to its laws. No measure of grief, however great, can leave us forever sensitive to the general suffering'' (The Gulag III, pp. 476-477).

We do not begrudge this great man his period of rehabilitation, some comforts after his terrible ordeal in the prisons. But afterwards, in his own ruthless self-criticism, he describes for us a frightful truth about prosperity: wealth, comfort, and entertainment, in all their multiple forms, act as a beautiful pink mist, a cocoon of cotton candy around the person, deadening our sensitivities to the "general suffering."

There is much talk today about "raising people's consciousness," sensitizing them to the needs of the world. One of the purposes of Christian asceticism is to do precisely that. (This is not its primary purpose but it can and should have that effect.) Information alone does not necessarily increase our concern for the needs of the world. Millions of people all year long read about and watch on television the tragedies of the world. This information may move some people to act; but I'm afraid for most, it propels them to spray more of the pink mist around, reinforce the cotton candy, immunize themselves from the harsh reality of the "general suffering."

There is something about experiencing the pain of the world *in our own bodies* which is the most conscience-raising method of all. It has often been suggested that when experts and delegates get together to discuss world hunger, instead of meeting at the Hilton, they meet in some abandoned warehouse and instead of lobster for dinner, they eat bread and water, like most of the poor they are discussing. This is not meant to be facetious. I think it would be the best possible arrangement for such a meeting.

Much of the fasting in the scriptures, especially in the prophets, has this dimension. It is not simply meant to purify the mind for prayer and the meeting with God. It has a definite social dimension. It makes people *aware* of their sins, or *aware* of coming disaster if they don't change their ways, or *aware* of the suffering of God's people.

Modern expressions of this are the hunger strikes in prisons (recall the ones in Ireland especially). Why do prisoners starve themselves? To drastically call the attention of the world to the suffering of others, to experience suffering in their own bodies so as to identify with others. Whatever you may think of these drastic measures, you must admit they certainly make us aware of the pain of others more than mere information could ever do.

For the Christian, ascetical practices like fasting are not done *merely* to heighten our consciousness. But it is one powerful way of breaking out of the pink mist and helping to blow the mist away from other people's eyes. Without this conscious effort (which Christian asceticism must be) the mist will not be dissipated. The laws of clay will take over. But we are in Christ. He has given us the power not to succumb to the numbing practices which immure us against reality.

So, if you really want to be concerned about the general suffering, start with your life-style. Allow the hunger, the poverty, the pain of the world to impinge on your own body. This is not to make you part of the problem but precisely to evaporate the pink mist of complacency and unreality so that your abilities, now sharpened and alive, can more generously respond to people's needs.

Night Duty

The priest-poustinikki at Madonna House presently have the service of night duty. It consists in turning out all the lights after everyone has gone back to their dorms, locking doors and, generally, putting the main house to bed. Despite its quite homey and practical character, there is something very priestly about it. It's like giving the final blessing to the day's activity and sealing the premises and the doors and windows against all nightly spectors. I kind of like it . . . now.

I say "now" because I haven't always appreciated it in the way I've just described. Now everything is neatly organized. Each priest is on for a two-week period and each of us has a schedule to follow. It wasn't always so. In the early, prehistorical period of priests doing night duty, schedules were a bit more "unspecified," shall we say.

Years ago I was assigned night duty on one occasion and I accepted it with the ordinary generosity of an ordinary member of Madonna House, consciously desiring to do my ordinary best. At the end of the two weeks I expected the change of duty in the ordinary way. It didn't happen. With a little extra-ordinary generosity I decided to "walk the extra mile" and not say anything. Two days passed, three. I started to fear that "something was wrong." At the end of the third week I panicked. Something *was* wrong!

It's possible that they had forgotten about the change of guard. Then I made (what I thought was) a really heroic decision. I would take on two periods in a row. During this fourth week I really was (I thought) being very generous; I was careful of thoughts of pride.

At the beginning of the fifth week began the first real temptation to inform somebody of what was happening. For some reason or another, this did not seem the thing to do. I felt God was about to teach me something valuable, so I thought I'd really abandon myself to his plans.

At the beginning of the sixth week I entered the first stages of denial. This is *not* happening to me! I was strongly tempted to tell somebody since it had now gone far enough. But, still, something within me said to wait, trust, abandon.

At the beginning of the seventh week, *anger* grew at those whose fault this was, coupled with a growing conviction that nobody really cared about me. (During the middle of this week, I was absolutely *convinced* that nobody cared about me!)

At the beginning of the eighth week, *forgiveness* of the

enemy surfaced, forgiveness for all those responsible.

At the beginning of the ninth week a general numbness set in and the absence of all noble, generous, forgiving sentiments. I experienced a state of negative indifference rather than positive, holy indifference.

It was not until the beginning of the tenth week that the first light concerning God's purpose in it all dawned on me. Why should my peace and happiness depend on this wholly external situation? Christ is my life. Christ is my peace.

God showed me very clearly that all these sources of unpeace were in my own heart and that is why I had to "submit," "forgive," "endure." It is the unfreedom in my own heart which gives the appearance that there are forces "out there" disturbing my peace. God said, "They are all in your own heart. If you accept that they are *in there* and abandon yourself to my will, I will give you real peace."

At the end of the eleventh week I began to enter a new realm of existence. It was no longer a negative acceptance. It was more of a positive living, not living through enduring but living in what was God's will for the moment. It was a new way of life, a taste of the kingdom.

It was sometime during the twelfth week that someone nonchalantly asked me, "How long have you been on night duty?" I said (and really, it was without any anger or malice or heroics; I had gone through all that), "Oh, about three months." A look of horror mingled with disbelief came over his face. "Three months!" he said. "Yes, three months." In such a situation he might have said, "Why didn't you say something," or "I'm sorry there was a mistake." And I might have said something silly like, "Oh, that's all right," or "I didn't mind." He just said, "Well, I'll get somebody else next week," and I just said, "Thanks." And I remember walking back to the poustinia, not in any virtuously triumphant way but quite humbled and quiet, because God had taught me a great secret, one I hope I never forget.

Making Prayer a Problem

I don't know about yourself but I have a tendency to turn everything into a problem. Gabriel Marcel said it beautifully, "Life is not a problem to be solved but a mystery to be lived." I wish I could live more like that. When people come to me, or ask to see me, I presume they have a problem. Instead of living simply in the presence of God, I try to figure out the "problem" of the active/contemplative life. I suppose we have to go through this phase of our lives being problems we must unravel. Hopefully it will only be a phase and not a permanent way of life. I want to share something of the phase I went through regarding prayer being a problem and the answer the Lord gave me.

The "problem" centers mostly around the question of why God doesn't hear our prayers. (Here I'm thinking of prayers concerning our own personal growth in love.) "Maybe God has favorites. Maybe I'm asking for the wrong thing. Maybe God is trying to teach me a lesson. Maybe, maybe, maybe."

One day I was meditating on the Gospel passage in which Jesus says we should keep on knocking, the passage in which he talks about the unjust judge and how much more will the Father give the Holy Spirit to those who ask him.

During that meditation another "maybe" came to light: "Maybe I don't desire enough what I ask for." And Jesus said, "That's it. That's the answer to your personal problem of prayer."

The key to the problem of prayer in our own personal spiritual life is a failure of desire. Jesus says to *keep on* asking, to *keep on* knocking. That kind of prayer always is heard. The Lord let me see very clearly that I don't really desire very deeply what I ask for. We must allow the whole weight and responsibility of our unanswered prayers to fall on *our own* heads, or hearts. As long as we continue to think it's God's problem, or some secret mystery of his dealings with us, these prayers for the conversion of our hearts will continue to go "unanswered."

By God's grace, I arrived at the point where I saw very, very clearly that I did not desire with any real depth what I was praying for. This may be the beginning of true prayer, when we realize and admit that we are in the presence of the King in a miserly, ungenerous state of soul — that we are actually terrified that God *may* hear our prayer! "My God, if I received more love, or the gift of tears, or more faith, it would revolutionize my whole life! Do I really want that?"

Why don't we persevere in our prayer? Because we are very ambivalent about actually getting what we're asking for. If we really wanted it, we would keep asking until we got it. We're actually afraid of getting it, so we don't keep asking . . . and then we turn it into a theological problem. We don't ask too long, for fear that God may hear us!

Now, we could be silly and ask further, "Well, why doesn't God give me the grace to desire more?" and thus enter into some infinitely complex "problem" of the mystery of grace and free will. But God in his mercy ended the discussion right there for me. I don't desire more because I'm lazy and ungenerous and don't love God very much. It's as simple . . . and awful . . . as that!

This is not a pleasant state to be in but there's something clear and real and even hopeful about it. Deep down I know it's in my power to have more of my prayers answered. It is no longer an intellectual problem, no longer a "Why?" shouted into the heavens. I know why and I weep over it. I wonder if I'm going to die like this, a man of small desires because I simply choose to be so. The wonderful part about this grace is the truth that on any given day, if I really want more love from God, he will absolutely give it to me. "Ask and you shall receive." I know the absolute truth of that promise. I weep because I don't *really ask.* God have mercy on me!

In Praise of Solitude

There is a very important (but unfortunately little-known) post-conciliar document called *"Venite Seorsum"* (Come Apart), of August 15, 1969. Its official, longer title is "Instruction on the Contemplative Life and on the Enclosure of Nuns." As far as I know, it is the Council's most powerful and pointed statement on the place of the life of solitude in the economy of salvation. I want simply to quote a number of passages from this document first of all, to emphasize the centrality of this way of life in the Body of Christ and secondly, to encourage you to read the document if you haven't already done so. Then I wish to make a few comments.

> Withdrawal from the world for the sake of leading a more intense life of prayer in solitude is nothing else than a particular way of living and expressing the paschal mystery of Christ, which is death ordained toward resurrection.

> To withdraw into the desert is for the Christian tantamount to associating himself more intimately with Christ's passion. . . . It was precisely on this account that monasteries were founded, situated as they are in the very heart of the mystery of Christ.

> Certainly the faithful are called to contribute . . . to the construction of the earthly city. . . . Yet with this mission the fulness of the mystery of the Church is not expressed, since the Church, though established for the service of God and man, is likewise — and even more especially — the aggregate of all who are redeemed, that is, of those who through Baptism and the other sacraments have already passed from this world to the Father. It is therefore both legitimate and necessary that some of Christ's followers . . . should give expres-

sion to this contemplative character of the Church by actually withdrawing into solitude. . . .

Monks and nuns . . . retiring to a cloistered life, put into practice in a more absolute and exemplary way an element essential to every Christian life: "From now on . . . let those who deal with the world (live) as if they had no dealings with it. For the form of this world is passing away."

. . . contemplative religious, bearing witness to the intimate life of the Church, are indispensable to the fulness of its presence.

And in a remarkable footnote by Pope John XXIII:

The contemplative life! . . . It constitutes one of the fundamental structures of the Holy Church, it has been present during all the phases of her bimillenary history.

One of my fantasies in the poustinia is giving rousing sermons on certain topics, knowing that I will probably never deliver such sermons. (Then again, in some instances I have given them. Maybe they aren't all fantasies. Maybe they're really from the Lord and I simply lack the courage to deliver them!)

One such homily would be a rousing call to solitude! I imagine myself a St. Jerome, who called young women to the life of virginity in his day and caused consternation among the noble Roman families! I have heard so much in my life about the "escape into solitude" that, armed with such documents as I've just quoted, I'd like to "go up on a high mountain" and shout, "IF SOLITUDE IS SUCH AN ESCAPE, WHY ARE SO FEW PEOPLE THERE!!!"

I think there always has been, there is now, and there always will be, a tremendous bias against the contemplative life, the life of solitude. Most people do not understand it at all. Many "tolerate it" because the Church approves it, but deep down they think it's a tremendous waste. I think there are very few people in the Church who positively appreciate it and pray that vocations to the contemplative life increase.

For years I have been hoping to read some rousing call to solitude, as we read so many rousing calls to action and social involvement. Imagine coming across an article entitled, "Come into Solitude and Live at the Center of the Mystery of Christ in the World!" Then I thought, "Maybe *I* should write such an article!"

I want to present to you a little syllogism. I don't say it's the Church's teaching but neither do I think its conclusion would be heretical. It goes like this: If most of the Church is in heaven ("the Church is more especially the aggregate of those who have passed from this world to the Father"), if the Church's deeper life is her contemplative, spiritual, interior aspect ("The Church is essentially both human and divine . . . but so constituted that in Her the human is directed to and subordinated to the divine, the visible to the invisible, action to contemplation, and this present world to that city yet to come . . ."), wouldn't it follow, then, that the Church's nature would be more fully expressed if more people were in solitude than engaged in activity?

Say there are 800,000,000 people in the Church. Would it really be a theological aberration (it certainly would be a sociological phenomenon!) if 400,000,000 were in solitude praying and 400,000,000 were engaged in activity? What would happen to the world if 400,000,000 people were praying in solitude!

Over the years as I've spoken to many religious who wish to enter into more solitude within their Orders but who met with much misunderstanding and resistance from their superiors. Why should the desire for solitude be under such a cloud, require so much discernment, be so suspect, be so extraordinary? Why can't it be more normal, more acceptable? Why does everybody have to fight so hard to get into solitude? Is it really an escape from activity? Is the apostolate so identified with active works that solitude cannot attain an equal appreciation? Why is there such a hassle to get into solitude?

I think many people in the Church need to admit their narrowness of vision here. The exalted value of a life apart is clearly recognized by the Church. We have a long way to go as far as the practical appreciation of this is concerned.

You Too Can Be a Saint

Consider the kind of men Jesus chose as his apostles. Not one of them "had it all together." It was the Lord's choice of *them* and their faithfulness to his choice which made them holy.

Every person is called by God to a unique, special and sublime mission in life. I use the words with great precision . . . unique, special, sublime. If we don't become saints it will be because, deep down in our hearts, we do not really believe we've been called. We may believe it for *some* others but we see our own hearts too closely and we know *we* don't have the goods.

You may look into your heart and see a great deal of pride and bravado . . . a loud mouth and no action. If so, go and talk it over with St. Peter. He knew what it was to have bravado and self-assurance turned into humble service and real courage.

You may look into your heart and see that you're on a glory trip in following Jesus, dominated by a "what's in it for me" attitude. If so, go and talk it over with the sons of thunder, James and John. They too were interested in status and privileges in the kingdom. They know how Jesus can transform glory trips into selfless dedication.

You may look into your heart and see a great attachment to money and material things and believe that God could not possibly use such a heart for anything so great as sanctity. If so, go and talk it over with St. Matthew. At one time he was probably planning to spend his whole life counting money he made from collecting taxes. He experienced how Jesus can transform miserliness into a spirit of evangelical poverty.

Perhaps you have spent part of your life (or are even now engaged) in hating God, or inflicting harm on the kingdom of God through ignorance or misguided zeal. If so, go and talk it over with St. Paul. He knows how Jesus forgives ignorance, how the Lord can completely change a person's life no matter how wrong he might have been.

Or, your faith may be very weak. If so, go and talk it over with St. Thomas. He knows all about it, how Christ can transform doubt and scepticism into an absolute faith that cries, "My Lord and my God!" The lives of these apostles and of all the saints prove that it's not our sins and weaknesses which are the dividing line between the saints and non-saints. All the saints were sinners; all the saints were saddled with certain weaknesses.

What is the dividing line, then? More grace? It is true, God is free to give more grace to some than to others. But this is not the determining factor. God wishes each of us to really be holy, to be saints. The determining factor is that, ultimately, *the saints believed more in God's power and his call than in their own powers and their own vision of life.* If we do not become holy, let's not rationalize it by saying that "I just wasn't chosen." You *have* been chosen! Your sins don't matter. The question is, do you have the courage to accept and live God's immense vision of life for you?

John Vianney and the Power of Prayer and Fasting

St. John Vianney is one of my great favorites. If you ever have a chance to go to Ars, don't miss the opportunity. It was one of the most inspiring places I've ever been. John Vianney used to spend twelve to fourteen hours a day in the confessional. (You weren't supposed to but I sat in his confessional for a few moments and prayed for the grace to be a good confessor in my own priesthood!)

There is one truth of the scriptures that was exemplified to a remarkable degree in the life of John Vianney. It is the power of prayer and fasting to change lives, even to change the course of history. God told Jonah to go to the people of Nineveh and tell them to fast and repent. "If the people listen, I shall relent, and not bring the disaster on them which I had intended for their misdeeds." The people did fast and repent, as we know, and disaster was avoided. Even if the Book of Jonah is a particular literary genre, the truth it graphically presents is found throughout the scriptures. Prayer and fasting can effect real changes in people's hearts, in historical events and even . . . it seems astounding to say so . . . in the plans of God. "I will not bring on them the disaster which I had intended." These "plans of disaster" God would rather not carry out. Mysteriously, we have an intercessory power to avert these consequences of our sins.

John Vianney said to God, during those long, nightly vigils of his, "God, I will pray and fast for these people if you will save them." God agreed. John Vianney prayed and fasted as few priests ever have for their people. And God saved them. Even to this day there is a special faith atmosphere in the village of Ars.

Imagine if somebody walked the streets of New York or Chicago or London or Toronto calling, "If everybody in this city fasts and prays, God will avert any serious harm from this city!" I'm sure that if everyone fasted and prayed, the future of that city would be different.

We have this power of intercession within us. Origen, I think, said that prayer is the greatest of human acts because it has power over God himself. God has given us this power but we don't really believe enough in it. If we did believe in it . . . actually believed that through our prayer and fasting we could effect beneficial changes in the

71

world . . . we certainly would pray more!

It is not only faith we lack but compassion for others as well. One of the secrets of true prayer is not method or technique or a certain acquired state of mind. One of the secrets is simply being concerned enough about people to pray for them.

When Moses was praying for hours during the battle with the Amelikites, he was not wondering what method to use! He was so concerned about his people that he just prayed his heart out for them and his prayer was heard. If we really believed, and had compassion for others, wouldn't we be praying and fasting more for them?

Surely, we've all experienced God answering our prayers at one time or another. We have to be careful we don't tend to deny it when he answers. There's a tendency in us to say, "Well, how do I know it was really *my prayers* that did it? It probably wasn't." This could be humility; it could also be my timidity in facing the fact that maybe it *was* my prayers! Because if it was . . . well, that means that I really do have this power. It increases my responsibility for using it. If God answered my prayers once, he probably can do it again. And then, there's no end to it! I'll have to pray all the time! Tomorrow there will be somebody else and the next day somebody else and the next day somebody else. It's a terribly responsible truth to face that *my prayers can effect real change.*

John Vianney prayed and fasted and helped to convert his people. We too have that same power within us. It's just that we don't have the same generosity. We theoretically believe it's possible; we just don't have enough compassion for the world. We really have no adequate notion of what happens when we talk to God. If we did, we certainly would talk to him more, intercede with him more, for all our brothers and sisters.

Thomas Aquinas, Patron of Those Tempted to Suicide

I don't know if there is a patron saint for those tempted to commit suicide but my choice would be Thomas Aquinas. This may strike you as strange. "What did he know of real life? Brought up in a monastic school, he spent all of his life reading and teaching and studying and writing. An ivory tower existence! Did he know any anguish at all??"

Aquinas is one of the greatest teachers and thinkers of all time. His greatness consists in the fact that he squarely faced all the agonizing questions of existence. The very first question of the *Summa* is, *"Utrum Deus Sit?"* "Does God Exist?" Then he goes on to ask thousands of other questions, most of which today we wouldn't even think of asking. Aquinas faced them all.

If he was a saint (which he was) it means that he just didn't deal with these questions in a purely theoretical fashion. He pounded them out in his heart and mind and body. In short, he *agonized* over them. And he was led by God to one of the most magnificent achievements of the human mind and heart.

Suicide stems from helplessness and meaninglessness. Aquinas paints for us, in his works, the magnificent panorama of the meaning of the universe . . . God, angels, the human person, sin, Christ, the Church, eternal life. To read his works is to be grounded in the realization that life not only has meaning but that there is truly *magnificent plan* and harmony to everything.

Jacques and Raissa Maritan once made a suicide pact. They agreed to kill themselves if within a year they could not find the truth. If life was meaningless, then there was no purpose in living it! They discovered the truth in Thomas Aquinas. Through his writings God won for the Church and for the modern world one of the greatest of contemporary thinkers and his gifted and holy wife.

73

When you are in a helpless and meaningless frame of mind, or really tempted to suicide by the absurdity of the world, pray to Thomas Aquinas. He became a reservoir of wisdom and hope and knowledge about God and the world. If Thomas was alive he would be grappling with all the great issues of our day. He would face them squarely and show how the truth of Christ is still supreme.

Nor would Thomas overpower you with his knowledge and answers. One day an elderly woman wrote and asked if there really was in heaven a book which contained the names of the just. She believed there was but some of her friends were denying it.

His reply is an indication of his wisdom and gentleness in not unduly disturbing the delicate consciences of the faithful. He wrote back, "It is my personal opinion that there is not such a book but if you wish to believe there is, I don't see any harm in it." He knew how to answer the important questions with clarity and firmness and how to respect the opinions of ordinary people in lesser matters.

When the world seems to be idiotic and meaningless and especially if you're tempted to suicide, pray to Thomas to reveal to you the splendor of all creation.

St. Joseph, Patron of Vocations

I don't know who the patron of vocations is but St. Joseph would be my choice. A vocation is first of all a call from God; secondly, it is being entrusted with a part of God's plan for the world.

In our schools and colleges there are what are called "Vocational Directors" and "Vocational Offices." You go to these people and they ask you what *you* would like to do with your life. Then, they may give you some tests to see if you have abilities for your preferred vocation. Or, the tests may reveal that you would be good doing something else. All this has some value but it is all quite centered on what *you* want, or what the *tests* say. Where is God in all this?

I'm sure Joseph had some of his own plans for his life. (Was carpentry really his preference, or something he fell back on when God's plan for him became clear?) But then this strange incident occurred concerning his betrothed. God broke into his life and changed all his plans. He probably thought his own plans (which he had prayed over, etc.) were from God, until he experienced a completely new and unusual call.

I think many people miss their real vocations because they have been too rational and programmed about it all. They do not allow enough scope to the grace of God, which often calls people to completely different vocations from what they imagined for themselves. To discover our true vocation, the first requirement is to be open to the surprise grace of God, as Joseph was.

Secondly, a vocation means that one is entrusted by God with a part of his plan for the world. It is not simply, or even primarily, a way of fulfilling ourselves. A true vocation is a dedication, a sense of being called to give our lives to some ideal or mission greater than ourselves, like Joseph.

Joseph had his own plans but God asked him to take care of the Savior of the world and his Mother. I'm sure his own holiness and fulfillment were not at the forefront of his consciousness. He was being called to totally dedicate his life to the care and protection of the Mother and Child. It was by giving himself to *that mission* that he himself became holy.

At the time of our saying yes, it may not be clear to us how we are going to come to God. But as we remain faithful, we experience that we are becoming holy by being faithful to the Lord's call, by being faithful to the part of the vineyard entrusted to us. It's a matter of breaking out of our own little plan for ourselves and allowing ourselves to be caught up in God's plan for us. It's a matter of almost not seeking directly our own development but the advancement of God's kingdom.

"St. Joseph, you who said yes to the Lord's breaking into your plans, you who dedicated your life to what God wished you to do, pray for all those seeking their true vocations!"

Holy Blackmail

One day someone came to see me. We talked for a while, then he went to confession. In the course of the confession he said that in a few days he was going to visit someone and commit sin. He knew it was sinful but he was going to go through with it anyway.

I remained silent and prayed. After a few moments I said, "I am not going to eat anything until you change your mind."

He got very nervous and upset and said, "You can't do that!" I said, "Yes, I can, and there's nothing you can do to stop me." After several other protestations, he left.

Two days later he came back and said, "Stop fasting. I won't do it."

Blackmail? Yes, in a way, but holy blackmail. "But," you say, "he stopped not so much out of love for God but to stop you from fasting." His love and concern for me was stronger than his love for sin, that's all. I just had to twist his arm a little. Blackmail? Yes, but holy, don't you think?

Praying for Our Ancestors

Christians have always prayed for the dead. We have an instinct which tells us that when the Lord comes at the moment of death, many people will not be ready to greet him. Not being ready, we sense that they will still need our prayers. What difficulties they may be in, or how long their predicament may last involves the various interpretations of the doctrine of purgatory. "It is a holy and wholesome thought to pray for the dead, that they may be loosed from their sins" (2 Mac. 12:46). The Church has always ratified this as a Spirit-inspired movement of the human heart. I would like to share with you something of what the Lord has been teaching a certain Dr. McAll. I think it lends a profound dimension to this whole area of praying for the deceased.

Dr. McAll presently lives in England and he is a fascinating man. He was born in China and Chinese is his first language. He comes from a long line of surgeon-missionaries. His father, grandfather and great-grandfather were all surgeon-missionaries in foreign countries to help heal the wounds of the world. Dr. McAll became a surgeon also.

After spending many years of his life caring for people's bodies, the Lord said to him one day, "Now I want you to learn everything science can teach you about the human *mind.*" So he went to England and became a psychiatrist, which he is now. Gradually, in his treatment of people, the Lord began to show him, little by little, some connections between difficulties people experience, and their ancestors.

One example he gives illustrates exactly what the Lord was teaching him.

A woman came to him once about her teenage boy who was engaged in the bizarre behavior of tieing up other children and beating them. Dr. McAll said, sort of matter-of-factly, "That sounds like a slave-driver." The mother said, surprised, "How did you know?" "Know what?" asked Dr. McAll. "That's the family curse," she said. "Our ancestors were slave-drivers who brought slaves from Africa."

Scripture says that the sins of the parents are visited upon the children to the third and fourth generation. This insight was one of the stages of revelation regarding the problem of evil. It is not personal sin, of course, just as original sin is not personal sin. We know a great deal about heredity today. We know that both disease and beneficial traits can be biologically passed on to children. And what about psychic traits? What about behavioral patterns due to sin?

This is a very mysterious area. Without attempting to rashly "figure out" all such connections, let us consider what the Lord led Dr. McAll to do. Besides the normal psychiatric procedures and besides the not-too-normal procedures (for psychiatrists, that is) of praying over people for healing, Dr. McAll was led to a still deeper connection, that of praying for the ancestors of people. (By the way, he became an Anglican because the denomination he belonged to did not believe in praying for the dead and had no service of prayer for the dead.)

In the case of the boy mentioned, Dr. McAll was led to draw up a family tree, with special emphasis on those who were involved in slave trading. He asked for the Eucharist to be celebrated for them and placed this family tree upon the altar. In this particular instance, the boy was completely healed of his compulsion.

Again, we are in a very mysterious area. It is not being suggested that a great deal of our personal problems are due to our ancestors. The point is that sometimes, in some areas of people's personalities, this may be the case. If our ancestors have died with burdens of sin and guilt still unresolved, our *prayers for them* may be the key to their own release into freedom, and ours.

In Dr. McAll's experience, a graphic example of this is the whole area of haunted houses. It's a statistical fact that often such houses have a history of past violent deaths, either murder or suicide. Dr. McAll asks a priest to go into the house and celebrate the Eucharist for the release of the person or persons who have died in the house. Very frequently, the disturbances cease. It's almost as if, by these disturbances, the dead are trying to get our attention. If this is true of such audible phenomena (noises, etc.), could it not also be true of the noises in our own psyches and spirits?

Could it be that a certain amount of the personal and societal disturbances we experience are due to the restlessness of the dead? Perhaps some of our personal disturbances are in reality "distress signals," calls for help from ancestors. Perhaps this is where, in part, our instinct to pray for the dead comes from. Through our human connectedness, we sense we are in some way praying for *ourselves*.

Along with the general loss of faith today there is a lack of faith in praying for the dead. At prayers of petitions during Mass, we very seldom hear people pray for the souls in purgatory. The point is that there are countless numbers of people who die *for whom no one prays*. Think of the tragedy of the thousands of abortions performed each day, the millions each year! Surely these children, deprived of life here, are resting securely in the heart of the Father. Consider, however, the psychic and spiritual carnage left behind in the parents and doctors and in everybody else connected with abortions. These people have killed human life; and these people responsible for abortions must face death themselves with this burden on their consciences. How much family, societal and personal disturbances are now due to the sin of abortion?

Perhaps you have ancestors you have never prayed for, or not very much. It's a wonderful practice, I think, and one which fits in very well with our whole understanding of praying for the dead, to make up a family tree and place it on the altar during the Eucharist. There may be long-standing problems in your family relations which the Lord wishes to heal through your prayers for your deceased ancestors. "It is a holy and wholesome thought to pray for the dead, that they may be loosed from their sins" and that *we* might be loosed from their sins also.

Abraham of the Broken Heart

Abraham is the father of all the faithful because he trusted in God. He is a man of immense spiritual stature in our history of salvation. But like so many of these outstanding people, we can tend to see their great faith or their great obedience apart from their real human struggle. The very succinctness of the scriptural texts can lead to such a misconception. "The Lord said to Abram, 'Go forth . . . ,' [and] Abram went as the Lord directed"; "God put Abraham to the test. 'Abraham!' 'Ready!' he replied. 'Take your son . . . and offer him up. . . . ' Early the next morning Abraham set out for the place of which God had told him." We have here the naked commands and responses but nothing of the human anguish involved.

The saints are great because their very sensitive humanities encountered the very absolute Word of God in a titanic struggle. The saints are not swept away by God's will in some effortless flow of generosity and ease. They do not dance lightly through all the harsh demands of the Spirit's breath upon them. They are great because they suffered their hearts to be broken over and over again, so that God might accomplish his important plans through them. Abraham is a good example.

First of all, God asked him to give up his homeland and never see it again. The text is simple . . . "Go! And Abraham went" . . . but what is the human struggle here? Home, country, place of origins, relatives, clan . . . these are among the most precious of human attachments. Abraham's heart must have been broken somewhat as he gathered all his possessions and family and set out for he did not know where.

When Abraham traveled into Gerar (Gen. 20), rightly or wrongly (wrongly as it turned out), he thought God was asking him to sacrifice even his beloved wife, Sarah. He told Sarah to say to Abimelech, the king, that she was his (Abraham's) sister. At the time, Abraham didn't see any other way out of what he thought was extreme danger to himself and his family. So he gave Sarah over to a pagan king. That night his heart must have been broken, to have given his dear wife to another.

Abraham had been promised an immense posterity by the Lord but he kept getting on in age and Sarah never became pregnant. It was not simply a matter of reaching forty-five or fifty or fifty-five. The text says, "Abraham was a hundred years old when his son Isaac was born to him." Imagine, all those years, waiting and hoping and wondering! Abraham's heart must have been constantly broken as he watched his servants and kinsmen enjoying their children and grandchildren while he and Sarah remained childless. His heart must have been broken.

And then, the breaking of all breaking, God commanding him to give up his only son, his only heir, "your only one, whom you love." The text implies that the word "Ready!" just leaped immediately, joyously, spontaneously out of Abraham's mouth.

But did it? Would it be less credit to Abraham if he struggled days or weeks with that command? Could anyone say yes to such a command in a moment? I don't think so. I think Abraham was filled with unimaginable terror and dread and sorrow at the thought. His great heart must have burst asunder when he finally said to God, "Ready!" Truly, his heart must have broken.

The text tells us that he journeyed three days into the wilderness. Imagine, journeying through the heat of the desert for three days with such a mission, such a burden, with such a broken heart! Was Abraham's heart "in it"? Yes, his heart was "in it" though he must have felt that it was no longer his own heart but rather, a heart which had been broken so many times he hardly recognized it. It was still his heart but so given over now to God's plan that his change of name from Abram to Abraham was not a fiction; he was a *new* person.

And then there was that unimaginable climb up the

81

mountain alone with Isaac. How can one climb a mountain with one's heart in pieces? Talk about laconic statements! We have that heart-rending, heart-breaking question of Isaac, "Father . . . where is the sheep for the holocaust?"

Did Abraham answer immediately? Could any really human person have answered immediately, as the text seems to imply? There must have been eons of silence and oceans of interior tears; then, finally, as if the breaking of a great dam . . . the final breaking open of Abraham's mighty heart, "Son, God himself will provide the sheep for the holocaust."

We know the happy ending of the story. God stopped Abraham from sacrificing his son, just as he gave back Abraham a homeland after he took the original one away, just as he gave Sarah back after Abraham handed her over to the king of Gerar and just as he gave Abraham children after making him live almost the whole of his life without any.

Why does God do these things? Is it because he is cruel, sadistic, likes to see us suffer? No, of course not. He does these things to his true servants because he is God. He knows that the possessions and people we think *are* our life, the things we believe we can never live without, the things which are, to us, the *most precious things in creation*, are *not* our life. God knows that *he* is our most precious possession.

So that our hearts might be capable of embracing him, possessing him, God must break them open again and again. By our little, miserly loves we constrict our hearts, actually rendering them incapable of the possession of God. And who would voluntarily break open his own heart? It is an act of God's mercy when he breaks them open. It may hurt him even more than it hurts us. It certainly hurt Jesus.

After our hearts are broken, they are never the same. When the angel held Abraham's arm, his heart did not return to its condition previous to the Lord's command.

The return of the gift did not wipe out the struggle to consent, the three-day journey through the desert, the terrible climb up the mountain. When we are given back our homeland, our wife, our son, it is never a return to our former state. Our hearts have been broken open.

If we have said, like Abraham, "Ready!" (even though through a million tears and heartaches) all precious things will be possessed now within a larger and more immense Precious Reality . . . God. We will still rejoice in our homeland, but it will be different. We will rejoice that our wife was not violated and that our son was not killed but it will be different. Everything will be ordered in God; our hearts will know what true preciousness is.

Then, the greatest blessing of all! What we experience as a broken and shattered heart will be revealed for what it really is. God has taken away our small heart and given us a heart capable of loving himself as he really is. The experience of this most precious love will make all the heartaches understandable and worthwhile.

This is certainly what Abraham experienced at the end of his life. He became a man "after God's own heart" because he trusted that the God who broke his heart was perfectly capable of putting it back together again. No, not putting it back together; it never really *was* together! What God did for Abraham was the most wonderful of all of his works. He gave Abraham a heart capable of an infinite love. It was worth all the breakings!

The Delicate Asceticism of Uriah

One day I was reading the Book of Samuel and came across this passage about Uriah. You will remember that David slept with Bathsheba, Uriah's wife; then David called Uriah back from the battlefield. After speaking with him, David told Uriah to go home and get some "rest" (no doubt hoping Uriah would have sexual relations with his wife, thus protecting David should Bathsheba be pregnant from him).

> But Uriah slept at the entrance of the royal palace with the other officers of his lord, and did not go down to his own house. David was told that Uriah had not gone home. So he said to Uriah, "Have you not come from a journey? Why, then, did you not go down to your house?" Uriah answered David, "The ark and Israel and Judah are lodged in tents, and my lord Joab and your majesty's servants are encamped in the open field. Can I go home to eat and to drink and to sleep with my wife? As the Lord lives and as you live, I will do no such thing" (2 Sam. 11:9-11).

What a wonderful, delicate attitude this is! How to describe it, what name to give it! It is one thing to fight alongside your brothers and share, when you are with them, all the same hardships of the struggle. This we call "comradeship" and "loyalty" and "patriotism." But when you are *away* from the battle and refuse comforts *because your brothers are still in the battle*, such an attitude goes beyond all the normal labels. What drew Uriah to such self-denial was a profound union with his brothers which physical distance and personal advantages and opportunities could not diminish.

In our attempts at personal asceticism, we need strong motivations. We know that we need to be detached from so many things but where to get the strength, the motivation, to do so?

We could pray for this "Uriah grace." Are you trying to be more detached from food? How can you stuff yourself when your brothers and sisters around the world are dying of hunger? You can't stand the monotony of your day? How can you complain when so many are suffering from unjust imprisonment, when so many poor must live drab lives due to the greed and oppression of others! For almost any cross in your own life that God is asking you to carry more courageously, if you just looked around the world . . . and often you don't have to look too far . . . you could see your brothers and sisters "lodged in tents," that is, suffering the very same things. Our deep oneness with them could draw forth from us added strength.

But Uriah's attitude was even deeper than all this. He wasn't thinking of his own ascetical program. He wasn't in any way using the sufferings of his brothers in the field "to become a better person." He wasn't thinking of that at all. Uriah simply had this amazing, caring solidarity with his brothers. His refusal to "eat and drink and sleep with his wife" flowed naturally and spontaneously from this oneness. It's a magnificent attitude, isn't it? St. Uriah, pray for us!

What Is a Prophet?

There is a renewal of prophecy in the Church today for which we should praise and thank God. "Do not despise prophecy," says Saint Paul. But along with true prophets there is a host of false prophets and also of people who mean well but whose spirit of prophecy comes more from human activity than from God.

What or who is a prophet? When I say the word "prophet," what do you think of? Is a prophet someone who foretells the future? Well, some prophets sometimes have foretold the future; Jesus foretold some things. But prophecy in its essence does not always contain this.

Is a prophet one who foretells coming disaster? Well, some prophets sometimes have foretold coming disasters; Jesus foretold some.

Is a prophet someone who criticizes the evils of society? Well, prophets sometimes do that, and Jesus did it also. (Today especially we have a host of people criticizing society and foretelling doom. Some of these people have a grace

85

from God to speak thus; most probably do not.)

Well, then, what is a prophet? For the answer we must turn to Jesus, the King of prophets. If we look closely at his basic teaching . . . every word of which was essentially prophetic . . . what do we find? Jesus is caught up in the vision of his Father's glory, his Father's love, his Father's plan for the world. He calls people to a change of heart so they can enter into his vision, into the kingdom of love and hope and consolation.

Jesus essentially doesn't go around preaching coming disaster, nor does he spend too much time condemning the evils of society. (In fact, if you look closely, you will see that he never criticizes abstract institutions like the Roman Empire or the system of taxation. Jesus always criticizes individual *people* who do evil things.)

Jesus already lives in the kingdom of his Father. Out of this vision, out of this consciousness, he preaches the present reality of the kingdom. He is on fire with the vision of what the Father is now presenting to his children. A prophet, therefore, is someone who has seen the glory of God, someone who has tasted the life of the kingdom . . . "the life of the world to come" . . . and who passionately calls people to enter into it. Real prophets have seen a vision of the glory of God. They have not simply gathered some terrible statistics on the present state of the world!

Listen again to what happened to two of the greatest prophets who ever lived, Isaiah and Ezechiel. "I saw the Lord seated on a high and lofty throne, with the train of his garment filling the temple, and seraphim were stationed above; each of them had six wings, and with two wings they veiled their faces, and with two they veiled their feet, and with two they hovered aloft. 'Holy, holy, holy is the Lord of Hosts,' they cried to one another."

Isaiah is the prophet of consolation and hope and these messages flow from his vision of God's glory.

About Ezechiel we read, "Above the firmament over their heads, something like a throne could be seen, looking like sapphire, and upon it was seated, up above, One who had the appearance of a man, and, like the bow which appears in the clouds on a rainy day, there was such splendor that surrounded him, such was the vision and the likeness of the glory of the Lord." Whatever Ezechiel had to say to the people of his time and to us, it flowed from his vision of the glory and majesty of God.

And what about John the Baptist, of whom Jesus said not a greater man had ever been born? We think of him sometimes as emerging from his desert condemning and castigating everything and everybody. He did have *some* harsh words to say! But if you look closely, he is basically a messenger of *hope*. He too has seen the vision of God in our very midst. "There is one among you whom you do not know. . . ." John is on fire with the vision of God's presence, God's plan of hope for his people. Only in the light of that wonderful vision did he warn and call people to repentance.

There are many people today calling themselves prophets, struggling to articulate the Word of God. A few of these really are prophets; however, I suspect many others are well-intentioned people struggling to be a voice for God but who are much too much caught up in their own human words and ideas.

What should we look for in a prophet? Look for somebody who has had a real vision of the glory of God. That will be a rare person. Look for somebody who has already tasted the present kingdom and speaks to us words of passionate hope even in the midst of the darkness. Look for somebody who is caught up in *God*, somebody who inspires enthusiasm for the things of *God*, somebody who calls us to live as *God* would have us live, somebody who *knows* that *God* is with his people and is perfectly capable of saving them.

We will not listen to people who simply say, "Peace! Peace!" when there is no peace. We will not listen to people who simply criticize our faults and the evils of society after reading the morning paper. We will not listen to people who only foretell doom and destruction.

But we *will* listen to somebody who is on fire with the vision of God's glory, the vision of his wonderful plan for us, someone who has tasted already the kingdom which is in our midst. Yes, such a person may also call us to repentance; we *should* repent. Yes, such a person may also foretell hard times ahead if we do not repent; harder times *will be* ahead if we don't repent! But only when such words proceed out of the vision of God's glory will they be life-giving; only then should we listen; only then, I think, will they be truly prophetic.

Do You Understand What I Have Done?

One Holy Thursday I was listening to the reading of the Passion. When it came to the part where Peter says, "Lord, you shall never wash my feet," the Spirit drew me into a meditation, into a dialogue between Peter and Jesus.

Peter sees Jesus getting up from the table and asking for a basin and towel. Then he sees him taking off his outer garment. Peter thinks to himself, "Oh, my God, he's going to wash our feet or something." Then he says to Jesus, "Lord, I understand what you're trying to do. You're trying to teach us something about humility and serving one another. You have often told us to wash each other's feet and we didn't. But we understand now! Really, there's no need for you to get down on your hands and knees and do this humiliating thing. Please don't! We understand!"

And Jesus says to him: "You don't understand! You don't serve one another and you don't wash each other's feet. You're still proud and want to be the big shots. There's no other way to break through your pride except by myself washing your feet. If you don't let me do this for you, you can have no part of me."

While he was in the garden with Jesus, Peter heard the

sounds of soldiers coming and he thought to himself, "Oh, my God, they're coming after him like a common criminal!" He turned and said to Jesus, "Lord, I know what you're trying to teach us. We are the criminals. We are the thieves and robbers. We are the ones who get away with all our crimes. But you, you are the Innocent One. Lord, we understand now. So you don't have to let yourself be taken like a common criminal! Please don't go through with this! We'll confess our crimes!"

Jesus said, "You *don't* understand. Yes, you are the thieves and robbers. You commit crimes in your hearts and get away with it. Real brigands go free and innocent people suffer. How can I get it across to you that there is great injustice in the world! The only way is to let you see Innocence Itself apprehended. Maybe then you'll see the injustice all around you! Unless you let me do this for you, you can have no part with me."

When Peter heard that Jesus was going to be scourged and beaten by the soldiers, he ran to him and said, "O Lord, please, please don't go through with this! Oh, please don't! I know what you are trying to say. We have offended your Father by our lusts and addictions and unruly appetites and now you're going to have your flesh torn apart to show what sin does to you. But Lord, we understand now. You don't have to go through with this! Please, please don't."

And Jesus said, "Peter, Peter. You don't understand. Unless I show you in my own flesh what sin does, you won't understand. So I'm going to have my flesh torn apart to make you realize how sins of the flesh disfigure the image of God. This is the only way to get through to you. Unless you let me do this for you, you can have no part with me!"

Peter saw that Jesus was going to carry a cross through the streets of Jerusalem. He ran up to Jesus and said, "O Lord, no, no, you can't go through with this! Don't drag your cross through the streets and the jeering crowds. We understand now, really we do. You have told us to carry our crosses every day, to carry each other's crosses. So we will. We promise. We will. You don't have to go this far. We'll obey you! We'll obey you!"

And Jesus said, "You won't obey. You won't carry your cross and the cross of one another. Your selfishness is too great. No. I must go through with this. I must show what it costs to carry one's cross. The human heart is too selfish, too self-centered. I must do this for you. If you don't let me do this for you, you can have no part with me."

Then Peter realized that Christ was actually going to be nailed to the cross. "Oh, my God, he's going to go through with this terrible tragedy!" Peter ran up to Jesus and said, "Lord, O my Lord, stop, stop! We understand! We understand! We will stop being selfish. We will lay down our lives in love for one another. O my Lord, please don't allow yourself to be killed. No, don't. We understand now."

Jesus said, "No, you don't understand. I'm telling you, unless you allow me to die for you, your heart never will be broken open. The wound of sin is too great, an 'incurable wound,' too massive. You have to see me, your Lord and God, die for you. It's the only thing that will break open the human heart. If you don't allow me to die for you, you can have no part with me."

My brothers and sisters, we must "let in" the passion of Jesus. There is a way we can block it out of our hearts and consciousness. There is a cry in our hearts that says, "No, no, no, you don't have to do that! Don't wash my feet, don't be scourged, don't be nailed to a cross! You don't have to go that far! Please don't!"

But he *has* done it and we must let it in, accept it, allow his passion to crack open our hearts. The "incurable wound" is too great. Jesus suffered his passion because it's the only way he could get through to us, make us realize what sin is. The passion is not only a revelation of love; it is a revelation of the darkness, of the magnitude of sin as well. We must allow Jesus to wash our feet and be scourged.

90

Let us even say to him, "Lord, if you must do it, then let the truth of your passion enter not only a small part of me . . . not only wash my feet . . . but Lord, let your passion enter my whole being so that none of your sufferings will be wasted. I see now that only by your wounds am I healed."

It's True!

I want to share with you one of the really deep graces I received during Lent a year ago.

In solitude you struggle with all kinds of thoughts . . . *logismoi*, as the desert fathers called them. Everybody struggles with them but solitude intensifies the combat. One cluster of such thoughts has to do with what other people think about your being in solitude. I went through several stages here, until the Lord graced me with the final stage of peace and truth. By stages, I don't mean chronological stages; perhaps "layers" would be a better term since each of these temptations or thoughts can be present on the same day. They are stages in the sense that one type predominates over another at certain times.

One layer of such thoughts deals with justifying your existence for being in solitude. It's an unusual life-style, so you yourself must come up with faith reasons for your being in solitude. You have permission to be in solitude; the Church has an exalted view of people praying in solitude so, basically, it is God's will that you are here. This is your first line of defense against temptations.

But still you struggle. What if others don't understand? What if they think you're lazy? What if they think you're avoiding work, or the active ministry? What if they think you are selfish, enjoying all that solitude when there is so much work to be done?

One way of handling these thoughts is to realize that you've no idea what people actually are thinking. Probably at any given moment, only you and God are thinking about yourself! You see clearly that these thoughts are your own projections but this doesn't stop them. For a while you live with this pain of fighting what you know are your own projections, literally fighting yourself. It's a mystery why they should persist even after you know they are your own projections! You must simply stand still in the midst of your own craziness and powerlessness.

But then, a new dimension is added. Somebody says it to you directly, or you hear it indirectly. Some people actually *do* have these thoughts about you! This is more terrifying. Now it is not a matter of your own projections, but of reality. So you pray for these people, forgive them, ask the Lord to enlighten them! You suffer these things now as a kind of martyr to solitude!

Finally, God in his mercy assists you to reach a deeper level. One day it became absolutely clear to me . . . and I was given the grace to accept it in my heart . . . I was given the grace to see that *it's true.*

What's true? It's true that I am lazy, selfish, avoiding work, avoiding people, deluding myself, etc. The Lord showed me that *I'm only bothered by such thoughts because they're truths in my own heart, they're part of me.*

I can't tell you what a freedom I've had since then. It became clear that one of the fruits of solitude is precisely to admit this basic level of sinfulness in which we live all the time. That's the only way I can describe it.

We say that baptism has taken away original sin but it seems that all our lives we will be in some state of sinfulness. We will never be able to say, "I'm not proud," or "I'm not lazy." I can never say that I'm not proud or lazy or selfish. I will be these things till my dying day.

So now I'm not bothered by those thoughts any more. Or rather, when they do arise, they no longer cause anxiety or unpeace. Now they add to a healthy sense of reality about myself. I no longer frantically try to get rid of them like wiping off mud after being splashed by a car. I can't really "get rid of" these thoughts. God has given me the grace to accept the truth of them, whether I think them of myself, or I think other people are thinking them of me. I think of them because they're true.

This is not some kind of fatalistic acceptance, "That's just the way I am so I have to live with it." No. I keep trying to be less selfish, less lazy, even though I realize that I can never totally eradicate selfishness and laziness altogether. That will never happen. Solitude exposes this basic nakedness so that one cannot avoid it. It's simply true. And I was given the grace to accept it about myself. If people are thinking those thoughts, they just see what is really in my heart. I *suspected* that these thoughts were true. Now I *know* that they are. And I am free.

With Unveiled Faces

As Moses came down from Mount Sinai with the two tablets of the commandments in his hands, he did not know that the skin of his face had become radiant while he conversed with the Lord (Ex. 35:29).

Teresa of Avila relates that one day she saw a vision of a person living a life of divine grace. She said that if she hadn't been sustained by the power of God, she would have died because of the overwhelming beauty of the vision. Moses' spirit too was radiant because of his conversations with the Lord and this brilliance was allowed to shine forth from his face. Moses only *spoke* with God. He was not aware of the indwelling presence of the Spirit, not aware of the mystery of the Blessed Trinity within him, not aware of God becoming a man. Moses did not receive every day the Body and Blood of his risen Lord.

My brothers and sisters, each one of us living the divine life is a dazzling universe of light. If it was allowed to break forth through our eyes and faces, no one could stand the

93

brilliance. The radiance of Moses' face is only an image of the radiance within the Christian. Teresa of Avila was allowed to catch a glimpse of it and it almost killed her, so majestic was its beauty.

"Moses did not know that the skin of his face had become radiant." We also are shining with great brilliance and we don't know it. The Trinity lives within us; we are temples of the Holy Spirit; Christ makes his home in us; we feed every day on his Body and Blood, speak with him face to face in an intimacy more profound than Moses on the mountain but, because of our lack of faith, we do not know that our faces are shining.

A further tragedy is that we do not see that radiance on the faces of our brothers and sisters. Ordinarily, when we approach each other, we are preoccupied with the other's sins or failures, the ways in which he or she differs from us. We are wrapped in our own fears that the other will not love us or like us. Jesus said the kingdom of God is within us. When two people meet, two magnificent kingdoms of grace are meeting; two little universes of dazzling light and radiance are coming together. But what occupies the center of our consciousness? Our hurts, our fears, our resentments, our projections, our anxieties!

Forget it all! Jesus says that when we find the kingdom, the pearl of great price, we should sell everything, get rid of everything in order to purchase it. So too when we meet our brothers and sisters, forget the past, the hurts, the sins. Forget yourself, your fears, your needs. Live by faith! See the radiance streaming from your own face and that of your brothers and sisters. Plough through all the psychological and emotional junk in between. Meet and embrace the pearl, the image of God, who is there before you.

"When Aaron, and the other Israelites saw Moses and noticed how radiant the skin of his face had become, they were afraid to come near him." Why are we afraid to approach the radiance of God shining through our brothers and sisters? Do we love the darkness more than the light? Do we think it is heroic to concentrate on each other's sins and failures and personal difficulties? No. That is easy. It would be heroic to enter into the radiance of each other's face.

St. Paul says that we gaze "on the Lord's glory with unveiled faces, [and] are being transformed from glory to glory into his very image by the Lord who is the Spirit" (2 Cor. 3:18). We too, my brothers and sisters, should be gazing at the unveiled faces of one another, so that in and through our relationships, we also can be transformed from glory to glory.

But we cover our faces with the veils of unforgiven sins and hurts, veils of resentments and projections, veils of fears and anxieties. Let us cast off these veils; cast them off not only when we go to speak with the Lord but especially in our relationships with one another. We no longer fear God; we love him. We should no longer fear one another but love one another without fear. Let us meet the unveiled faces and bask in the hidden but real radiance which streams from each other's face.

Jesus and Mary

Jesus' relationship with women is a delicate topic. Nikos Kazantazkis was excommunicated from the Orthodox Church for his handling of the theme in *The Last Temptation of Christ*. Of late there have been several blasphemous movies on the subject. For all that . . . for all the obvious dangers and extravagances, for all the unavoidable human projections of our own onto the relationship . . . for all that, there must be some delicate, Spirit-guided way of entering into this beautiful aspect of the Lord's life.

There is so little in the gospels, really. We know that women traveled with Jesus and were part of his company.

95

We know that Jesus must have been a most attractive human being. Thousands of meditations have been written about the woman of Samaria coming to the well on that hot afternoon. She saw Jesus there before she approached. What was she really thinking? What was she really desiring?

"Mary" in the preceding title refers to Mary of Magdala. What do we really know about her? We're not even sure she was the woman who washed Jesus' feet and dried them with her hair. We do know that he drove some demons out of her and forgave her sins; we do know that she was in this close company of women who traveled with him; we do know she was at the foot of the cross; we do know that he appeared to her in the garden on that first glorious morning. This is what we know from the scriptures.

But there are all the in-between spaces. He must have known her for more than a year. They must have often talked together. The scene in the garden shows us something of the intensity of Mary's love for Jesus.

There is much written today about celibate love. I think one of the deepest sources of wisdom about celibate love is to be found in Jesus' Heart, in that place where he related to Mary of Magdala. To enter Jesus' Heart and be instructed by his Spirit concerning his attitudes and dispositions is the place of ultimate truth for the Christian. We have his life and words in the gospels; we are joined to him by his Spirit. It is this Spirit teaching us from within Christ's Heart which is the source of all light for us.

It is not so much a question of entering Mary's heart. Mary did not become a saint overnight! She had been, if we may presume, a great lover of men. She was human like us. Her forgiveness and conversion did not magically change her into a Teresa of Avila! Great as Mary was, her heart was still probably quite confused as to how to love this Man in a new way. So, it is into the Heart of Christ we must plunge to discover the beauty and strength and purity of celibate love.

Each man and woman must do this for himself or herself. Each person is struggling to love purely according to his or her vocation. Each person will have different questions to ask. But if we ask them of the Heart of Christ and enter through his Spirit into his relationship with Mary, we will be enlightened about pure love, holy love, celibate love.

All I wish to do here is share with you some of the questions I asked the Lord; maybe some day I will share more of the answers I received. But they will be my answers. I think the exciting and important point is that each person enter Jesus' wonderful relationship with Mary Magdalene and ask his or her own questions. Here are some that I asked.

"Lord Jesus, what was your relationship with Mary Magdalene? We need to know, Lord, as we're trying to love each other purely and simply as your children, as men and women living with your new life."

"After Mary washed your feet and you forgave her sins, did *you* invite her to join your close circle of friends, or did *she* ask you if she could? I can imagine either way. She might have been too ashamed of her past and thought too little of herself to ask for such a thing. And yet, she loved you so much. I can imagine her just starting to be around you and you understanding and accepting it without any words spoken between you."

"She was with you for at least a year, perhaps longer. Did you ever talk alone together, and what did you talk about? Did she ask about your life in Nazareth and did you tell her about your Mother and about other women you had known in Nazareth?"

"Did you think she was beautiful and did you ever tell her so? Did Mary ever say "romantic" things to you and how did you respond? How did you teach her what true love was? Was her obvious love and affection for you ever a cause for murmuring and snide remarks on the part of

97

others? And how did you respond to *that?*"

"How did you think of Mary, Lord, I mean in your mind and heart? I don't ask out of curiosity but because I really need to know. We want to think and relate to one another purely and simply, as you did with Mary."

"Did you think of her sometimes more than others? In your humanness, did you like to be with her more than others? You must have been a very gracious and attractive person, Jesus! How did you, in your speech and actions, constantly keep directing her towards the deeper love of your Father? Was she hard to teach? Was her sinful past a great obstacle to overcome; or was she such a great lover that she was able quickly to learn the art of divine loving?"

"She probably wanted to do many little things for you. Did you let her? Or did you have to say no sometimes in order to guide her loving; or did she know herself how to be lovingly sensitive?"

"Was her presence at the foot of the cross a special consolation for you? Were you grateful she was there?"

"Lord, you appeared to Mary first of all after your resurrection. Was she there because her love brought her to the garden, or did you bring her to the garden because you desired so much to see her?"

"In your long journey through death and back again, did you think of Mary in any special way?"

"In the gospel of your servant John it says that Mary clung to you. Lord, was she holding onto your feet, or did she throw her arms around you and press you to her breast? You had to tell her to release you, Lord, but how long did you let her hold you? How long did you hold *her?*"

"Did you have some special conversations with her before you returned to your Father? And when you left the earth, Lord, did you miss her?"

"Lord, we do not ask these questions out of curiosity, or in any way to pull you down to our often too human ways of relating. But we know that you were a man and she was a woman and that you both loved each other very much.

We too are men and women and we want to love each other as you loved Mary Magdalene. So we ask these questions because we really need to know. Help us to enter this wonderful place in your Heart where you related purely to Mary and by your love created such a magnificent human being!"

God Is the Silence

I cry out and there is no response, I moan and there is no reply.

We have all done it: cried out to God for help, for a word of guidance, for a sense of his presence and received in return only *silence*. The Lord has shown me that *he himself is the silence*. What we thought was a critical state of anxiety or helplessness was a blessing in disguise. It was God's way of clearing out our hearts so his Presence in the silence could come pouring through. But we didn't recognize him.

Although I had experienced God as silence in prayer, it wasn't until I came across a fascinating description of different ways of knowing God in the writings of Karl Rahner that a whole new dimension of this truth became clear to me. Unfortunately I have misplaced the reference in Rahner but I remember well the kernel of his thought.

He said that much of the traditional understanding of the degrees of prayer is built upon a Greek notion of knowledge. There is an ascending scale of purer and purer concepts in Greek thought. There are thoughts of physical realities, then the abstractions of mathematics, then pure concepts of philosophy . . . being, truth, etc. Then, in the suspension of all thought, one reaches the "purest state of the mind," being completely void of all material or rational conceptions. This is the Greek view.

But this is only one particular theory of knowledge. You might simply ask why is it more perfect to think "being" than to think "cow"? If you were trying to get away from matter, this would be reasonable. But what if you're not trying to get away from matter? What if you're like St. Anthony of the desert, who said that when he prayed he would just go outside, look at the beauties of the universe and praise God for them? For the Christian, there is no reason to say that looking at a rose and praising God is less perfect than closing your eyes and praising God without any other thought in your head. For the Christian, the more perfect prayer depends on the love in the heart, not the content of the mind.

Rahner says there's another possible theory. Instead of locating God at the apex of this hierarchy of concepts, so that you don't really "reach him" until you are free from material conceptions, look at it a different way. See God not at the end of a ladder but as the one who makes all knowledge possible, the one who forms the background to all our knowing, whether a rose or a philosophical concept.

Whenever we are thinking of anything . . . and even when we might be in an imageless, thought-less state of mind, these thoughts, these states are always against a background like the words on this page are on the background of the page. The images are on a background of silence, just as the thought-less state is also on a background of silence. Rahner says that God is this constant background, this always-present silence. If you just close your eyes for a moment and consider this background, you will see what I mean.

A few days after reading this I was at prayer. This "background" of silence became so vividly for me the presence of God that I cried out loud, "Oh, Father!" so close did God seem! It only lasted for a moment.

Since then I have come across this same idea in several other places. In Max Picard's *The World of Silence*, he says, "The silence of God is different from the silence of men. It is not opposed to the word: word and silence are one in God. Just as language constitutes the nature of man,

100

so silence is the nature of God.'' Picard quotes Wilhelm Vischer:

> The voice of God is not a voice of nature or of all voices of nature put together, but the voice of silence. As certainly as the whole of creation would be dumb if the Lord had not given it the power of speech and as certainly as everything that hath breath should therefore praise the Lord, just as certainly only he hears in all voices the voice of the Lord Himself, who hears the voice that is inaudible.

I may be over-reacting here, or perhaps I have just personally discovered a truth that everybody has known all along, but for me, the implications of the statement ''God's nature is silence,'' and the implications of Rahner's refocusing of the place we apprehend God in our knowing, are astounding, wonderful! I really don't know what superlatives to use! I hope this isn't heretical but in my own prayer life it's as if I now touch the constant presence of God in this ever-present background of silence.

This background is always there. Whether you're at peace or anxious or in pain, whatever is happening, it is always happening against this background of silence. And this silence is the nature of God as we ordinarily apprehend it. Being human, we want God to be a word, or a pleasant sensation, a satisfaction of some kind. In a way, silence, the ever-present silence, is all of these . . . only word/satisfaction/pleasure in a different mode. I have discovered that it's possible to enter ever more deeply into the reality of this silence and it doesn't even depend upon physical silence, although this can be a better context. Even if noise and sound are present there is always this silence which forms the background to everything and this silence is God's nature as part of our constant experience.

All this, of course, is in the Christian context. Picard says beautifully that it was out of mercy that God broke his silence and spoke to us in Jesus. Jesus now reveals God to us. When Lao-tse said, "Silence is the great revelation," he did not know that this Silence was Father, Son and Holy Spirit. We know the mystery behind the silence but the Silence is still there, ever-present, as a medicine.

In my experience, it's possible to focus upon this ever-present Silence, behind which there is no other silence. It's a wonder to me why there is not an indefinite "silence behind silence behind silence," but there isn't. I think this is the merciful presence of God himself in our consciousness.

Honesty and Sincerity

One of the distortions of modern life is the abuse of words; this flows, of course, from the abuse and misunderstanding of the reality to which they refer. "Love" is at the top of everyone's abuse of words list. My second choice would be honesty and sincerity.

I was born in 1936. If I was simply asked what honesty as a virtue meant as I was growing up, I would say it meant "not telling lies, not cheating on exams or while playing basketball, being truthful about your sins in confession." (Note: All these examples implied a standard against which honesty could be measured. There *was* truth, there *were* rules for the game, there *were* morally sinful actions about which we were all sure.) Sincerity meant that you tried to have your speech and actions correspond with your spoken word. It was akin to truthfulness. Of course, we always knew one could be "sincerely wrong," but this always implied you could find out the truth and correct your ignorance. In short, the words honesty and sincerity always implied some objective content to which I had to conform so I could be honest.

While I was still growing, a new concept of honesty and sincerity was growing in the world. It was being fostered by many factors but especially by Freudianism.

In the privacy of psychoanalytic sessions (whose methods more and more began spilling over into the rest of our lives) honesty and sincerity were coming to mean *mere talking about what was happening inside of one.* There was no longer any relationship between truth or morality and the word honesty. *It was honest merely because it was said.* To hold back something you were thinking was *dishonest.* In other words, honesty had lost any relationship to objective standards. Statements (and eventually actions) were not honest because they conformed to some standard; they were now honest because you did not restrain yourself from saying (or doing) them. It was honesty without any form.

Honesty now means to say what you think. It used to mean the struggle to say truthful things, loving things. If you said something harmful, you were sorry for it and tried not to say it again. The new virtue is not putting any restraint on speech. Such restraint is considered "dishonest and insincere." The new honesty is saying what you think no matter what it is, as long as it's what you really think, what is "really going on inside of you." If you don't communicate what is really going on inside of you, you're dishonest.

This new virtue is a complete reversal of another virtue from my own upbringing: tact. "Tact" comes from the word "to touch." It's a sensitivity to the inner being of another, how to relate to people without hurting them. It's a respect for the inner sanctuary of another, allowing a sphere of personal privacy to remain around the sanctuary of their heart.

There is no respect for this mystery now. Everything is to be exposed. And the way to expose it is by endless talking and conversation. Many conversations in the modern world are two people "honestly and sincerely" pouring their naked worlds into one another. If this were happening between two deep friends, it might be a virtue. But people are doing it indiscriminately to anybody, often using

103

this "honest method" expecially towards people they dislike!

People are "honestly and sincerely" saying all kinds of terrible things to one another without any qualms of conscience, because, according to the new ethic, they are not really doing anything wrong. The wrong thing (if any standard is admitted) would be to repress any of the things they are sincerely thinking!

The desert fathers and countless generations before them were well aware of the harmful, crazy, terrible thoughts within each man . . . but they never thought it a virtue to *say* them! The virtue was in *restraining* them. The unanimous testimony of the scriptures is for restraint, conforming our speech and actions to the laws of charity. Now, restraint is the *vice*. Jesus said love one another, not "be honest with one another" in this modern sense. "Letting it all out" is not love. Reverence and tact and respect and restraining ourselves from saying harmful things have always been what charity is all about.

Honest Christian conversation is not the spewing forth of endless streams of conscious and subconscious thoughts upon one another. Jesus says that if anybody calls his brother a fool — simpleton, dumb-bell — he will be guilty of hell-fire. This is an infinite distance from the new ethic. We can't help thinking such thoughts sometimes, but nowhere in the scriptures are we encouraged to *say* them. We're supposed to ask God's grace, first of all to change our hearts so we don't think such thoughts; and secondly, even if we do think them, to give us the loving restraint not to *say* them.

When Christians communicate it is the meeting of two infinite worlds of persons. Most of this personhood lies in mystery. The tact and silence and restraint with which we approach one another is respect for the mystery. The modern "honest" approach destroys the mystery — rapes it. It tries to get at the "real person" which is conceived to be all the conscious, subconscious, and unconscious stuff inside. St. Paul says, "Speak the truth in love." This is a far cry from the new honesty.

Unpacking

I experience silence as essential to my being as air is to my body, but I cannot always say why. I believe silence is essential for everybody, although they may not know it. Every once in a while I read something which articulates for me part of the reason for my need for silence, a word which lifts part of the veil of the essential place silence has in our lives.

The following insight is from G.K. Chesterton's *The Well and the Shadows,* in a chapter appropriately entitled "The Case for Hermits":

> There is a strong case for more solitude; especially now that there is really no solitude. The reason why even the normal human being should be half a hermit is that it is the only way in which his mind can have a half-holiday. It is the only way to get any fun even out of the facts of life; yes, even if the facts are games and dances and operas. It bears most resemblance to the unpacking of luggage. It has been said that we live on a railway station; many of us live in a luggage van; or wander about the world with luggage that we never unpack at all. For the best things that happen to us are those we get out of what has already happened. If men were honest with themselves, they would agree that actual social engagements, even with those they love, often seem strangely brief, breathless, thwarted or inconclusive. Mere society is a way of turning friends into acquaintances. The real profit is not in meeting our friends, but in having met them. Now when people merely plunge from crush to crush,

and from crowd to crowd, they never discover the positive joy of life. They are like men always hungry, because their food never digests.

Recall some occasion when you returned from a rather long trip. You are very tired. You are loaded down with suitcases and a motley assortment of bags of every shape and size. Your pockets are filled with souvenirs, money, packages of gum, bits of paper with addresses and directions. Your mind and heart are loaded down also with a multitude of new experiences — places you've been and people you've met. Often we are too tired to unpack on arrival. We just collapse in a chair or bed and say we will unpack in the morning, or when we get a chance.

Chesterton says life is like that. Each day is filled with a multitude of experiences which need unpacking. He says more; he actually says that the unpacking is the better part. "The *best* things that happen to us are those we get out of what has already happened." "The real profit is not in meeting our friends, but in having met them."

It is an extremely important question put to each of us whether we believe this or not. It may first of all strike us as a quaint insight into human existence but its implications are vast and far-reaching. He is saying that without silence, without the unpacking of our experiences, we are simply half alive. We are missing the best part of all. When you return from that trip, the best part is still ahead of you. You will be spending many hours quietly assimilating all you have experienced. There will be the telling of stories and the showing of pictures (even if you bore your friends with them!). Beyond that, there will be the lifetime settling of all these experiences into your being, like a stone dropping gently to the bottom of a lake.

The poet Wallace Stevens wrote: "I do not know which to prefer, the beauty of inflections or the beauty of innuendoes, the blackbird whistling or just after."

Which is the richer experience, a wonderful time spent

with your best friend, or just after? The listening to a beautiful symphony, or just after?

We could call this silent aspect of life's experiences "savoring." It is not an accidental or optional aspect of life but an essential component. Obviously we cannot achieve a silent unpacking of every experience. This is not possible and not what is meant. But in a given day or week or month there are experiences which are new, or crucial, traumatic or vital to our lives. If they are not "unpacked" they remain "mere" experiences. We speak about "superficial experiences." Of their nature they are momentary and fragmentary. An essential component of life is silence and solitude, in order to digest and assimilate what has happened.

Why is the experience of reading in silence, contemplating a work of art in silence, watching a sunset in silence, sitting in silence with a loved one, so extraordinarily beautiful and enriching? It is because in these experiences we have both the outward experience and the savoring, happening simultaneously. This is not true of most of our experiences. Where do we acquire the savoring of these experiences, the "existential depth," the assimilation into our deepest being? In silence, in solitude. Only reflective silence, through remembering and imagining and a kind of spiritual tasting, can our experiences become integrated with the self.

Of course, we do not wish to "savor" all of our experiences. Many of our experiences during the day have been confusing or even harmful. But this too is an essential part of the unpacking. After a vacation we often regret having wasted precious time through wrong decisions, or having gone to uninteresting places. We say, "I'm never going there again," or, "We're never going to see them again." Especially in the modern world where there is so much noise and a welter of harmful experiences, we need the silence to *prevent* certain experiences from entering our deeper being. We need to positively reject many of them and make decisions "not to go there again." Without this unpacking of our experiences, our consciousness remains a jumble of superficial impressions. This can only lead to a great disorientation in the person, or rather, to a positive prevention of true personality ever developing. Personhood has something to do with depth of experience. Without unpacking ... without silence and solitude ... there can be no depth.

I don't think we can underestimate the absolute necessity of unpacking. Much of the modern mentality and practice seems built on the premise that one grows and matures through a multiplicity of experiences; the more experiences one has, the more mature, and the more a "person" one becomes. There would be more truth to this attitude if silence were included as one of the experiences. But often silence, in the sense of positive unpacking and reflection, has no place in the modern world. Life then is like eating without digesting, traveling and merely seeing things without any comprehension for one's life, listening to a song bird without relishing the "just after."

I suppose what I have been describing is simply one dimension of what we have always known as "recollection." This silent recollection is missing from many people's lives in the modern world. Life has become a kaleidoscope of mere experiences. There is no existential depth, no assimilation, no unpacking. Even the evenings which used to be man's time for quiet and the savoring of the day, even evenings are simply filled with more audio and visual experiences.

The precious moments just before sleep arrives. What should be a time for savoring par excellence become merely a negative separation from stimulation until sleep is over and the collecting of impressions begins again.

In such a world, people are only half alive, with not even the better half. We absolutely must have both dimensions in our lives — the whistling of the blackbird, and the silent moments just after.

Are You at Home with Yourself?

If anyone loves me, he will keep my words, and my Father will love him, and we will come to him and make our home with him.

God delights to make his home in each of us; he likes to be there. Do we? Do we delight to live in our own homes, our own hearts? In the Acts of the Apostles, Peter had a vision wherein he was asked to eat of all the different foods of the earth. "Not me, Lord," he said, "I'm not going to eat anything that's unclean."

"Don't call unclean what I have made," said the Lord.

The culmination of the gospel is an invitation from God to dwell completely in our own home, in our own hearts. But we say, "Oh no, Lord, I'm not going to live in such an unclean place, in such low-class housing."

"Don't call a place I delight to dwell in, poor housing," says the Lord.

The disorientation of ourselves from ourselves could be described as a fear, a loathing even, to dwell in all the rooms of our own house. There are many rooms within us and we have not really entered them all. The Good News is that God dwells in every one of those rooms; he really delights to be there. You can't venture any place into your heart where God is not present.

The Good News is that the Trinity dwells within us, makes their home within us. We have a deep longing to be at home with ourselves, not to run away from our personal solitude. Wouldn't it be wonderful to be at home with ourselves? We can be; it is the Lord's will that it be so. Only believe that Jesus himself delights to be in you. How can any room in your heart be fearful or dirty or loathsome if it is the throne room of the King!

Believe My Witness

At the end of Mark's Gospel Jesus tells the disciples to "go out to the whole world and proclaim the good news to all creatures." This means that it is part of God's plan that we believe those who witness to his deeds. After his resurrection, Jesus did not appear to everyone, only to those he chose beforehand. Then he said, "Go and tell my brothers this," or, "go and tell them that." The Gospel is meant to be spread by our *believing the witnessing of others.*

This is a very important aspect of our faith. When people try to witness to what God has done in their lives, we sometimes tend to say, "Well, that may be all well and good for them but I've never experienced God that way." Or, we may disbelieve entirely what the person is telling us.

Why don't we believe others when they tell us about the workings of God in their lives? I think we are sometimes jealous or sad that the graces they have received have not been given to us.

The Lord does different things to different people and he wants us to share what he has done so that we can all profit from each others experiences. After all, the whole Christian message is something we've received from those who have gone before us. Why don't we continue to believe in the many little revelations the Lord gives to each of us?

The Christian body is not a group of isolated individuals all receiving private insights, prophetic words and touches of the Spirit. We are all members of the same Body, receiving graces and little resurrection experiences which are meant to be shared.

Jesus often chided his apostles for not believing the witnesses he sent to them. A person who shared with us something wonderful that has happened to him or her just may have been sent to us by the Lord. Even if the person is overenthusiastic(!) let us "rejoice with those who rejoice." Let us believe one another. What God says to me is also for you and vice versa. If someone comes to us in joy to share the deeds of the Lord, let us not turn a disinterested ear. Yes, we need discernment. Yes, we should not be naive or gullible. But above all let us be careful of unbelief, jealousy, or pride. Let us believe in the witnesses of the Lord.

The Resurrection

In one sense the resurrection of Christ is one of the many truths listed in the Creed . . . "the third day he arose again from the dead." It is part of a long list of truths. But in a very, very important sense, we Christians only believe all the other truths *because* Christ has risen from the dead.

Before the resurrection of Jesus, the apostles believed in God, more or less. They believed, more or less, that Israel was the chosen people. They believed that Jesus certainly was a great prophet and some might even have believed that he was the Messiah . . . believed it more or less. Perhaps they believed in life after death. But when Jesus rose from the dead, all these truths that were believed with hesitation were now believed with an absoluteness which made their faith unconquerable.

Thus, the resurrection of Jesus is the central fact of our faith, the truth which gives solidity to everything else. You could, on your own, work out a proof for the existence of God and accept his reality, or you could do research into the history of religions and accept life after death because many other peoples do. But all this would not be specifically Christian. We believe in God as our Father and as One who cares for us because that is what Jesus preached and taught . . . and he came back from the dead to confirm his vision of life. We believe in life after death and all the other truths of our faith precisely because Jesus taught them and because Jesus has risen from the dead.

In our life together, what we should say more and more to one another and emphasize is that Jesus *is alive*. It is with this truth we should fight all our temptations. If you are tempted to disbelieve in God, say loudly in your heart, "Christ is risen!" If you are attacked by Satan, shout at him, "Christ is risen!" If you are speaking with someone who is discouraged and in despair, say to him or her, "Christ is risen!"

This is the cry of victory we should be repeating to ourselves and others over and over again. For us, the resurrection is our affirmation of life; it's not just another truth among many. Paul says that if Christ is not risen, our faith is nothing, empty. But Christ *is* risen! Therefore, God loves us and our sins are forgiven. We shall live forever and the devil is conquered . . . all because Christ is truly risen.

Of course, the big difference between the apostles and us is that they really *did* see the risen Lord, whereas we have not. We have to accept it on their testimony. Yet, in Mark's gospel, there is a very interesting progression of appearances.

Why didn't Jesus appear to the apostles first? Why did he appear to others — the women — and instruct them to go and tell the apostles? Wouldn't you think that if he was going to entrust the preaching of the resurrection to the apostles, he would have appeared to them first of all?

It was just the opposite. Jesus began by asking the apostles to believe in his resurrection on the testimony of others. Perhaps he did it that way so that they could experience the struggle of faith. After all, they were going to ask others to accept the resurrection on *their* testimony.

Perhaps there is another reason also. Jesus reprimanded them for not accepting the testimony of the women. I think he was speaking to all of them when he said, "You believe because you have seen. Blessed are those who have not seen and yet believed."

This is pure speculation on my part but could Jesus have been planning *not* to appear to the apostles, hoping that they would believe in his resurrection purely on the strength of his word that he would do so? He told them he was going to rise from the dead. According to the Lord's own word, it is a deeper faith to believe when we have not seen.

It is not recorded that Jesus appeared to his mother. Many meditations down through the ages imagine that he did. But I wonder. It's more blessed to believe without seeing. Mary is the great woman of faith. As Georgette Blaquiere has written, Mary is not among the myrrh-bearing women of Easter morning. She does not seek the living among the dead. I think that Mary didn't *need* to see an actual appearance of Jesus.

Even before she had heard the rumors that "he was alive," Mary, all during Holy Saturday, *was the Church,* absolutely certain that Jesus was the Messiah and that the Father would be faithful to him. By faith, she was united with Jesus in a way and to a depth that no actual appearance could increase. She was content to wait for heaven, so that she could continue to be the woman of faith, a strength for us in our own period of waiting.

Therefore, we should not be sad that we have not actually seen the risen Lord. We have his life, his words and above all the confirmation of the Spirit in our hearts. By believing in Jesus we experience his risen life in our attitudes, in our relationships, in every part of our being. Is not this proof enough for us? "Blessed are those who have not seen. . . ."

Jesus' Power to Save Is Utterly Certain

The power of Jesus to save is utterly certain, since he is living forever, interceding for all who come to God through him. Jesus is standing right now before the Father with his shining wounds. He has passed through everything that we will ever have to go through. He has, thereby, won for us the power to be saved. God wants each of us to have an incredible realization of the power of Jesus to save.

In the Gospel, Jesus says to the evil spirits, "Be quiet," and they are quiet. There are storms on the lake and he says, "Be still," and there is calm.

In our own lives there are storms still raging. There are darknesses where we feel the light of Christ has not yet penetrated. Fears keep us from moving ahead into God. As I was meditating on all this one day, I had a kind of imaginative vision.

I was standing on a road that was brilliantly lit up with the sun. It was a very long road . . . the course of my life. I was just starting out and I had a blindfold on. Because of the blindfold I could only take little baby steps, fearfully and timidly. I stepped on a few twigs and thought, "Oh, my goodness, I'm heading into a forest!" I inched a little further and stepped into a small ditch and thought, "Help, I'm going over a cliff!"

Then in my mind's eye I saw Jesus standing next to me. He said, "I will be your eyes on your journey. All you have to do is give me your hand and allow me to lead you. Don't let your fears prevent you from traveling life's road. What you call the forests and abysses are not really so; besides, they are nothing to me. They are products of your own fears. I have crossed over every abyss, gone through every dark forest, calmed every storm. I have passed through everything you fear. Come with me. Don't be afraid."

Here we are, all inching our way along the road of life. If our hand was really in the hand of Christ, we would be able to walk briskly, run even.

The power of Jesus to save is utterly certain but we must put ourselves in his hands, allow him to guide us. We must believe in his vision, in his strength. Otherwise, we will only be able to walk by our own feeble light, and we will not get very far. We will break a twig and think we are crashing through a forest, step into a little hole and think we are heading for the abyss. Christ is at our side. Let us trust him.

Psalm for a Night Vigil

One of the prayer-themes in scripture is that the night time is one of the best times for prayer and meditation. Jesus told us in a parable that the Bridegroom came at midnight. I've collected some texts on this theme; it is a beautiful prayer to say during the night. I thought I'd share it with you.

Come, bless the Lord, all you servants of the Lord, who stand in the house of the Lord during the hours of the night (134:1).

Where can I go from your spirit? From your presence where can I flee? . . . If I say, "Surely the darkness shall hide me, and night shall be my light" — For you darkness itself is not dark, and night shines as the day. (Darkness and light are the same) (139:7, 11, 12).

When I lie down in sleep, I wake again, for the Lord sustains me (3:6).

My soul yearns for you in the night; yes, my spirit within me keeps vigil for you (Is. 26:9).

I will remember you upon my couch, and through the night watches I will meditate on you (63:7).

O my God, you brighten the darkness about me (18:29).

My eyes greet the night watches in meditation on your promises (119:148).

Happy the man . . . who meditates on his law day and night (1:2).

Though you test my heart, searching it in the night, though you try me with fire, you shall find no malice (17:3).

My soul waits for the Lord, more than sentinels wait for the dawn (130:6).

By night I remember your name, O Lord, and I will keep your law (119:55).

Awake! Why are you asleep, O Lord? Arise! Cast us not off forever (44:24).

He neither sleeps nor slumbers, the guardian of Israel (121:4).

At midnight I rise to give you thanks (119: 62).

O God, I cry out by day, and you answer not; by night, and there is no relief for me (22:3).

You shall not fear the terror of the night, nor the pestilence that roams in darkness (91:5).

It is good to give thanks to you, O Lord, to sing praise to your name, Most High. To proclaim your kindness at dawn, and your faithfulness throughout the night (92:2).

By day the Lord bestows his grace, and at night I have his song, a prayer to my living God (42:9).

For his anger lasts but a moment; a lifetime his good will. At nightfall, weeping enters in, but with the dawn, rejoicing (30:6).

There is a stream whose runlets gladden the city of God, the holy dwelling of the Most High. God is in its midst; it shall not be disturbed; God will help it at the break of dawn (46:5-6).

Awake, O my soul; awake, lyre and harp! I will wake the dawn (57:9).

I will sing of your strength and revel at dawn in your kindness (59:17).

More than sentinels wait for the dawn, let Israel

wait for the Lord. For with the Lord is kindness and with him is plenteous redemption; he will redeem Israel from all their iniquities (130:7-8).

Fill us at daybreak with your kindness, that we may shout for joy and gladness all our days (90:14).

Rising in the middle of the night to watch and pray with the Lord is a profound and wonderful act of devotion. Try it sometime!

Helping Other People Love Me

In one of his instructions to his monks, St. Bernard told them, *"Ut studeas amare et amari"* . . . which freely translated means, "Have a care not only to love but to be loved as well." When I read this I had an insight as to what this admonition meant for me; I do not presume to say it is what Bernard meant.

What it said to me was, "Don't get so caught up in your own spiritual program of trying to love others that you fail to see the ways you make it difficult for *them to love you."* By "ways" I am not thinking first and foremost of my sins, although certainly these. But what characteristics, what personality quirks, preferences, ways of moving, likes and dislikes . . . in short, what do I do or not do that makes it harder for my sisters and brothers to love me? I had never quite asked myself that question before.

St. Paul said that he tried to become all things to all men. Part of loving has to do with being sensitive to the likes and dislikes of others to which I can conform, within limits, so that loving between me and others is facilitated. Some people like jokes but you don't particularly care for them. Would it really damage your spiritual development to break down and joke once in a while? Others are very talkative and you like to be reserved. Would it really set you back in your spirituality if you made an effort to join in more? Other examples could be multipled.

We all have an image of ourselves, a conscious identity, which we carry around in us all the time and according to which we relate and act. Others must relate to *my* identity and image. If not, well, that's the cross each of us must carry! But really, living the Gospel is our true identity; love is our true image. Love of the Gospel will keep forcing us out of our narrow conceptions of who we are. I think we cling to many superficial conceptions of who we are. I think we cling to many superficial characteristics of our "identity," which makes it more difficult for others to love us. We should break out of these self-imposed confines.

But isn't this wishy-washy love? St. Francis prayed, ". . . not so much to be loved as to love." The attitude I am speaking about here really is mostly concerned with the other. It is not a weak, compromising, unprincipled adaptation to everyone out of a need *we have* to be loved. It is really other-centered. It is a strong kind of love, secure enough in the love of God that it doesn't need to hold on, for dear life, to a superficial identity. "Amari!": the flexibility, born of a Gospel love, which enables us to bend in our relationships with others so as to make their efforts to love us a bit easier.

Is this taking away the cross? Don't worry! If we are sincerely trying to follow Christ, crosses there will be. But are some painful aspects of our relationships with others due to an unwillingness, conscious or unconscious, to let go of some of our superficial personal characteristics? Are there some ways I can make *me* not so hard to love?

Death, Judgment, Heaven and Hell

The 13th chapter of Mark's gospel belongs to a biblical form of literature called "apocalyptic." It is a Greek word which means "to remove the veil"; the Latin word "revelare" . . . revelation . . . means the same thing.

Remove the veil from *what?* The last act, you might say, of the human drama. God's people are asking the question, "What's it going to be like in the end? What is the last act of the play?" As Christians, we believe that Jesus Christ, in his life and work, raised the curtain on the last act. You might say we are in the scenes of the final act. But what is the final scene going to be like? This is where Christian theology talks about "the last things" . . . death, judgment, heaven and hell.

One thing is certain and it's at the heart of our faith: God will win in the end. The final victory of Christ is the meaning of the resurrection. In faith we believe that God's truth, God's justice, God's mercy will triumph. This emphasis is important. Thank God it is not our own small, limited, miserly conceptions that I am talking about but the truth and mercy and justice that are in God's heart. It is God's righteousness that I want to triumph; I believe it will certainly do so.

I'd like to speak about the realities of death, judgment, heaven and hell which form part of our thinking about the end of all things. I'd like to talk, not so much about these realities themselves, as how to think about them generally, how to relate them to our life with God.

The first thing to remember is that everything Jesus told us, whether it is harsh or not, is meant to be life-giving. Let's face it, we get very nervous, scared even, when we think about the last things. Except for heaven, they are not pleasant topics. They are very sobering, reminding us of life's ultimate truths. And probably all of us have some poor or inadequate formation to overcome as regards these truths of faith. But we *must* think upon these truths; they are part of our faith-understanding of reality. But what we need to do is think about them in a life-giving way.

When Jesus says, "This is my Body," the truth is life-giving, and we rejoice at it. When he says, "Come, you blessed of my Father," our hearts light up and we are filled with a wonderful hope. When he says, "I am the vine and

119

you are the branches," we experience a surge of confidence running through us because he chose to be so near to us. We hear all these words as words of life.

But, my brothers and sisters, when Jesus says, "You brood of vipers, who shall save you from the retribution to come," those are words of life too. And when Jesus says, "Depart from me, you cursed, into everlasting fire," those are words of life. Jesus means these harsh words to be life-giving as well, to help bring his people to the Father. It is very important that we help each other understand just how this can be so.

One of the differences (among many others) between Jesus talking about these truths and our talking about them is that Jesus always knew how to fit his words to his listeners. Jesus did not call the little poor people sitting on the hillsides a "brood of vipers, " nor did he ever say to the Pharisees, "Come, you blessed of my Father." Jesus had the genius for speaking the right truth to the right person at the right time.

When we talk about or teach these "last things," we often say the wrong thing to the wrong person at the wrong time. We tell little children about the horrors of hell fire and to those who are in sin and need to hear about it, we say nothing, or "Don't worry. Everything will be all right. God is merciful and in the end everything will be fine." Because of our lack of sensitivity, or insight, or courage, we often do not know how to speak about these "last things" in a life-giving way. We often simply "teach the doctrine" without adapting it (not watering it down but adapting it) to young or old, sinners or lovers of God.

Secondly, as Christians joined to Christ, we are already living in the new creation. Because of our lack of faith, we often talk and think about the last things as if we were still "strangers and aliens," and not already members of the kingdom.

Yes, physical death still awaits us and we have fears and apprehensions about it. But we have already undergone the radical death, the passage from death to life, "because we love the brethren." It is the death to sin that is the really wrenching experience. Now, through grace and our own efforts, we continue to die daily to sin. Little by little Jesus is preparing us for physical death. It probably will not be as terrible as we imagine. In thinking and speaking about death, let us remember we have already died with Christ and are already living the life of the resurrection.

Yes, a judgment awaits us but St. Paul says that "for those who are in Christ Jesus there is no longer any condemnation." This means that if you have accepted Christ and you are really trying to love him and do what he says, the judgment upon our lives has already happened. So we're not approaching a terrible Judge; we're approaching the Father who loves us and who is calling us into his kingdom.

Heaven. We probably don't have too much of a problem with heaven except that we do not allow ourselves to think of it and be encouraged by it as much as we should. These days, to talk and preach about heaven seems to make people feel guilty about and disloyal to their tasks upon earth. When is the last time you heard an inspiring sermon on heaven? We need to allow the reality of heaven to give us hope for life.

No doubt the concept of hell gives us all the most difficulty and it is on this I want to elaborate somewhat.

I would like to caution you when thinking upon the last things and especially about hell. Let's admit our ignorance: we really don't know an awful lot about these things. We need to have a great humility here. And above all we need to guard our minds lest the harshness of these realities (compounded by our ignorance) lead us to unfaithful and harsh attitudes towards God.

Because we don't know or fully understand judgment, we must be careful of projecting on God our own harsh images of judgment. Admit that you don't understand how to judge the human heart, nor how God will judge it. Be careful of saying, "God is unjust! God is a frightful Judge! God likes to punish people!" The devil can use all this to warp our whole understanding of who God is. God is always Father, always loving and whatever true justice is, we know that the Father will exercise it and it will be the most loving thing.

We all have problems with hell. Let's admit that we really don't understand sin, what it is for someone to have had the opportunity to love God and then refuse that opportunity. Let us admit that we really don't understand what it is for someone to reject God's Son, consciously and willfully. Let us admit that we don't understand what it is for someone to take the Blood of Jesus and throw it back in the Father's face. Let us admit that we don't understand, and beware of taking it out on God! "God is a sadist! God is Evil! God doesn't understand the weakness of the creatures he has made!" These are thoughts that come from hell itself.

There are many people, my brothers and sisters, who *do* refuse the love of God. There are many people who turn their hearts from God. Sometimes, because of our own faith, or because God has already given us a foretaste of joy and everlasting life, we can fail to appreciate the serious state that some other people are in. I think there are a lot of people whose eternal salvation is in jeopardy.

This is what Jesus is trying to say when he tells us those things about the sheep and the goats. He's trying to wake people up: "Listen! If there's something really wrong with your life you must change it. My Father takes your choices very seriously. God is not a fool; God is not a patsy; God is not a big lollipop in the sky." Yes, God is merciful but there's going to come a moment of truth for all of us and we have to face it. We have to have the courage to face the consequences of our actions. We know that is true, deep in our hearts.

We must be careful about watering down these truths

about the last things. Jesus talks about everlasting punishment. It's not easy to even entertain such a notion. But let's not say in our hearts, "Well, that's true, in the Gospel Jesus talks about it, but a merciful God could never allow such a thing. After a few million years or so God will put an end to it and we'll all live happily ever after." Because of our ignorance, we must be careful both of doing away with the hard truth altogether, or of coming up with really awful concepts of God.

We water down heaven too! "The eye has not seen, nor ear heard, nor has it entered into the heart of man what God has prepared for those who love him." Because of our small minds and hearts, not even heaven excites us or attracts us. "Heaven! Oh my goodness, it sounds kind of dull. Just sitting around and looking at God all day!" See how ignorant we are! We have no idea of what it will be like to see face to face the One who made us. How really dull *we* are! The Book of Revelation tells of the myriads of people who will be there . . . all the lovers of God of all times and places. What a wonderful and exciting place heaven will be! But, alas, we water down heaven too, and make the delights of God so much smaller than they will be.

Death, judgment, heaven, hell . . . how is it going to be in the end? Jesus will win . . . but it will be *Jesus' truth, Jesus' mercy, Jesus' love* that will win and thank God, not our own!

Everlasting Life

In all our thinking, willing, desiring, in every attitude and affection, we are called to "put on Christ," "to have the mind that was in Christ Jesus." Our faith is that, at least to some degree, this is possible for us. St. Paul says that no one knows the spirit of man except that man himself; and no one knows the mind of God except the Spirit of God.

123

Then he says an amazing thing: "But you have the mind of Christ." It is the Father's will that we become like his Son.

I would like to ask you to meditate for a moment upon that aspect of the Lord's awareness we call everlasting life. In the Creed we say we believe in "life everlasting." We know that this everlasting life is, in the first instance, God himself. "This is everlasting life, to know you, the one true God. . . . " The Second Person of the Trinity always lived this life, from all eternity, while he was on earth and he continues to live it forever and ever. There was never any interruption in this life of the Trinity. I would like to call your attention to the dimension of that life we refer to when we say "life everlasting," that is, life after death.

Much of the emphasis today is on "realized eschatology," that is, that our everlasting life begins right now. This is certainly true. However, there seems to be very little emphasis on heaven, on the reality of life after death. Not in the sense that we don't believe in it; we certainly do. But it seems there's a way in which we emphasize more *life here below* than the life we will live forever.

As in so many aspects of the psychology of Christ, it is a bit presumptuous to ask what was the Lord's awareness concerning life everlasting. St Paul assures us we can know the mind of Christ, so let us inquire about his awareness of time.

In St. John's gospel Jesus attests to his awareness of having been sent from the Father, of having come "from above," of having "descended from heaven." He has an awareness, then, of coming from some unimaginable, dimensionless expanse of eternity. Have you ever seen those atomic clocks in museums? The twelve hours represent the possible known existence of the universe. The hands of the clock are close to twelve, representing the brief known existence of homo sapiens. In terms of this clock, the life of one 70- or 80-year-old person could hardly be represented, so brief a span is it.

Try to imagine, then, the consciousness of earth-time of the Second Person of the Trinity, coming from eternity — spending 33 years here and returning to eternity. Can we describe the briefness, the transitoriness of Christ's awareness? Some brief flash on an eternal consciousness. Our individual lives also are just such brief flashes, although, because of our earth-boundness, our experience is much different. Our awareness is often that we're going to be *here* forever and sometimes we'd rather have it that way! My question is, do we strive to attain a consciousness of eternity such as the Lord must have had?

I think there are many factors militating against our striving after and desiring such as attitude. When was the last time you meditated on heaven, or everlasting life, or asked for the deepening of your longing for eternal life? I believe that our life in Christ will be deficient if we do not have something of Christ's consciousness of eternity, something of his longing to see the Father.

What hinders this longing? For one thing, earth is the only home we've ever known. Unlike Jesus, we haven't come from above, haven't descended from heaven. The earth *is* beautiful. Will there be trees and skies and mountains and lakes in heaven? Something in us hopes so. A natural love of the earth keeps us here.

Everlasting life is an existence even more beautiful. Our lack of faith makes us cling to the earth in the wrong way. We do not allow the greatness of our destiny to grow within us. Destined for everlasting life, we keep trying to build utopia here but it keeps slipping out of our hands. The longing for everlasting life does not grow in us because we refuse to rise to our greater dignity as heavenly destined people rather than earth-bound mortals.

Such language as "heavenly destined people" is very unpopular today, because the main thrust is "building the earth," securing justice and peace and material goods for all the peoples of the earth. Longing for everlasting life seems to be a disloyalty to the earthly enterprise. "There the

Christians go again! Gazing heavenward and neglecting the earth. Marx was right. Religion dulls people's responsibility towards the earth. They put up with injustice waiting for the pie in the sky.''

This is a gross distortion of what the longing for everlasting life was in Jesus and of what it should be in the Christian. If the longing to return to the Father was part of Jesus' consciousness, then it must form part of our consciousness as well. If it blinds us to the earthly demands of love, then it is not the consciousness of Jesus. If it causes us to sit around waiting for heaven, it is not the consciousness of Jesus either. That there is a real temptation and danger that the longing for eternal life can be used as a cop-out from a life of love is absolutely true; but that this is the *necessary* result of such a longing is absolutely false.

We have only to look at the lives of the saints to disprove this. No people have spent themselves as generously in the service of others as the saints. Yet, the saints were at the same time consumed with the desire to be with Christ. St. Paul was torn between dying and being with Christ and remaining on earth for the good of his people.

The truth is that a genuine, strong, realistic desire to see God and live forever is the only awareness that can really put all our earthly efforts into proper perspective. Jesus *always* had an immense desire to return to the Father; and yet, it in no way impoverished his concern for the earth. Don't let anyone tell you that such a desire is a cop-out from earthly existence! On the contrary, such a desire would add a terrific intensity to our earthly loves and concerns.

In the first place, if we really believed we would live forever, we would work much harder to ensure that all our brothers and sisters would enjoy the same life. The lack of a strong belief in everlasting life actually blinds us, and tends to make a certain amount of our activity a hindrance to attaining this life. It would keep our efforts in building

126

the earthly cities in perspective. Jesus said there are people building more and more barns for their material goods and that such people are fools. They could die tomorrow and then what would be the point of all their labor?

A solid belief and desire for everlasting life would release a tremendous amount of energy in us, paradoxical as this may sound. It's not the true desire for heaven which paralyzes us, but the fear of death. We use a lot of energy to immunize us from the reality of the shortness of this life. Again, the saints are our witness. *Because* they were detached from the earth, they could expend all their energies helping people in the right ways, ways that would not hinder their immortal souls.

This deep desire for everlasting life would make us live more in the truth. It's simply true that the earth *is* passing away. That's one of the things Jesus tried to tell us. Our hearts cannot rest in anything here below. Again, it doesn't mean that we don't try to infuse the life of Christ into everything on earth, seeking with all our strength to restore it to him so he can present it to the Father. But we cannot put our heart in these things. They will never make us happy. We cannot go about the restoration of the world to Christ giving the impression that we are building the eternal city right here.

When St. Paul exhorts you, "If you have risen with Christ, seek the things that are above where Christ is," don't feel guilty about seeking the things that are above. Don't let the misguided voices of the world lay a guilt trip on you, saying that you are a second-class citizen of the earth because of your gazing into the heavens. If our heart is really centered in Christ, centered in his longing to see the Father, no one will love the earth with greater or truer passion than we.

Let us stir up in one another a passionate desire for eternal life — and not feel guilty about it! It's not a betrayal of the earth but a cry to be loyal to the earth in the light of eternity.

Additional books from

LIVING FLAME PRESS

Order from your bookstore or
direct from Living Flame Press

JOURNEY INTO CONTEMPLATION $3.95

George A. Maloney, S.J. An in-depth handbook of guidance, inspiration and concrete advice. In it, Father Maloney provides sure teachings on deep union with God, discussing techniques, problems and anticipated rewards. Small groups who pray together contemplatively are also counseled. The author is a master retreat director and writer of many books, including our *The Returning Sun.*

MANNA IN THE DESERT $5.95

George A. Maloney, S.J. The Israelites spent 40 years wandering in the desert, a model of an indeterminate time for all Christians to spend in meeting God in the inner poverty of the desert of our hearts.

This book builds this theme using as a title the words Jesus used to describe Himself as the manna that has come down from heaven to feed hungry Christians in their desert journey to the heavenly Jerusalem. It is a book dealing with contemplative prayer and aims at Christians who have already begun the journey into contemplation. It touches on themes of a desert spirituality such as death-resurrection; weeping and mourning; silence and purification of the senses; prayer as adoration and as entering into the heart of Christ. It challenges growth of the *anima,* the Mary in us, especially as we encounter the crises of limits in our desert journey.

BECOMING A CHRISTIAN PERSON $5.95

Robert E. Lauder. Becoming a Christian person is a lifelong process. The author sees two elements as essential to that process; accepting the Father's love for us and reaching out in loving service to others. Exploring the implications of these two elements, Fr. Lauder discusses the mystery of personal existence, the meaning of death, the significance of the cross in the life of a Christian, the meaning of conscience and the necessity of prayer. All these topics are centered around the theme of Christian personhood.

LOVE IN ACTION $5.95
Reflections on Christian Service

Bernard Hayes, C.R. This book explores the spiritual base out of which all valid ministry must come. Very often, "doing" and "ministering" call for activity which is identical or similar. The difference between doing and ministering lies in the motive behind the activity. One can "do" for many reasons. One can "minister" only out of love. Using the gospel of John, we focus vividly and compellingly on the "why" of Jesus' ministering and we explore the explicit commissioning of the disciples to minister.

FINDING PEACE IN PAIN $3.50
The Reflections of a Christian Psychotherapist

Yvonne C. Hebert, M.A., M.F.C.C. This book offers a positive approach to overcome the paralyzing effects of emotional hurt in difficult life situations which can't be avoided or changed. Each of the ten chapters clearly illustrates how this form of special prayer can transform life's hurts into opportunities for emotional and spiritual growth. Ms. Hebert draws the reader into the real-life situations of those whom she counsels to join their pain to the sufferings of Christ in His passion.

THIRSTING FOR GOD IN SCRIPTURE $2.95

James McCaffrey, D.C.D. In this book, the author directs our attention to the Bible as a means of slaking that thirst, as a true source of light for the searching mind and heart. Several texts of Scripture are quoted at length and discussed. The copious references from other texts, not quoted, enable the reader to compare and contrast for him/herself the ways of the Spirit. It is by reading the Bible text itself that the truth and comfort of God's Word may sink into our lives.

PRAYING WITH MARY $3.50

Msgr. David E. Rosage. This handy little volume offers twenty-four short meditations or contemplations on the key events in the life of our Blessed Mother. The presentation is short, simple and to the point. The object is to turn the user to the New Testament so that he or she can bask in the light of God's Word, grow in love of that Word and respond to it as fully as possible. For a growing insight into Mary's interior life, these short reflections can be very helpful. *Reign of the Sacred Heart.*

RECONCILIATION: $5.95
The Sacramental Path to Peace

Msgr. David E. Rosage. Many of life's problems stem from strained or fragmented interpersonal relationships caused by anger, pride, jealousy, self-centeredness, etc. We may not readily recognize these causes since we have lost our sense of sin. In this book we gain insight into the merciful heart of Jesus which leads us to appreciate more fully the Sacrament of Penance as a channel of forgiveness and healing and peace.

SPIRITUAL DIRECTION $5.95
Contemporary Readings

Edited by Kevin Culligan, O.C.D. The revitalized ministry of spiritual direction is one of the surest signs of renewal in today's church. In this book seventeen leading writers and spiritual directors discuss history, meaning, demands and practice of this ministry. Readers of the book should include not just a spiritual elite, but the entire church — men and women, clergy and laity, members of religious communities.

ENCOUNTERING THE LORD $4.50
IN DAILY LIFE

Msgr. David E. Rosage. Delightfully spiced with humor and full of wisdom, this book is intended for all who would like to follow St. Paul's admonition to "pray constantly" but who "don't have time." The author helps us turn the mundane actions of life — sipping a cup of coffee, the exhilaration of jogging or the anonymity of an elevator ride — into food for prayer. The book also has quotations from Scripture which focus on the chapter and can carry through to our daily lives.

THE RETURNING SUN $2.50
Hope for a Broken World

George A. Maloney, S.J. In this collection of meditations, the author draws on his own experiences rooted in Eastern Christianity to aid the reader to enter into the world of the "heart." It is hoped that through contemplation of this material he/she will discover the return of the inextinguishable Sun of the universe, Jesus Christ, in a new and more experiential way.

BREAD FOR THE EATING $3.50

Kelly B. Kelly. Sequal to the popular *Grains of Wheat,* this small book of words received in prayer draws the reader closer to God through the imagery of wheat being processed into bread. The author shares her love of the natural world.

LIVING HERE AND HEREAFTER $2.95
Christian Dying, Death and Resurrection

Msgr. David E. Rosage. The author offers great comfort to us by dispelling our fears and anxieties about our life after this earthly sojourn. Based on God's Word as presented in Sacred Scripture, these brief daily meditations help us understand more clearly and deeply the meaning of suffering and death.

PRAYING WITH SCRIPTURE $3.95
IN THE HOLY LAND
Daily Meditations With the Risen Jesus

Msgr. David E. Rosage. Herein is offered a daily meeting with the Risen Jesus in those Holy Places which He sanctified by His human presence. Three hundred and sixty-five Scripture texts are selected and blended with the pilgrimage experiences of the author, a retreat master, and well-known writer on prayer.

DISCERNMENT: $3.50
Seeking God in Every Situation

Rev. Chris Aridas. "Many Christians struggle with ways to seek, know and understand God's plan for their lives. This book is prayerful, refreshing and very practical for daily application. It is one to be read and used regularly, not just read" *(Ray Roh, O.S.B.).*

DISCOVERING $3.95
PATHWAYS TO PRAYER

Msgr. David E. Rosage. Following Jesus was never meant to be dull, or worse, just duty-filled. Those who would aspire to a life of prayer and those who have already begun, will find this book amazingly thorough in its Scripture-punctuated approach.

"A simple but profound book which explains the many ways and forms of prayer by which the person hungering for closer union with God may find Him" *(Emmanuel Spillane, O.C.S.O., Abbot, Our Lady of the Holy Trinity Abbey, Huntsville, Utah).*

MOURNING: $2.95
THE HEALING JOURNEY

Rev. Kenneth J. Zanca. Comfort for those who have lost a loved one. Out of the grief suffered in the loss of both parents within two months, this young priest has written a sensitive, sympathetic yet humanly constructive book to help others who have lost loved ones. This is a book that might be given to the newly bereaved.

THE BORN-AGAIN CATHOLIC $4.95

Albert H. Boudreau. This book presents an authoritative imprimatur treatment of today's most interesting religious issue. The author, a Catholic layman, looks at church tradition past and present and shows that the born-again experience is not only valid, but actually is Catholic Christianity at its best. The exciting experience is not only investigated, but the reader is guided into revitalizing his or her own Christian experience. The informal style, colorful personal experiences, and helpful diagrams make this book enjoyable and profitable reading.

WISDOM INSTRUCTS HER CHILDREN $3.95
The Power of the Spirit and the Word

John Randall, S.T.D. The author believes that now is God's time for "wisdom." Through the Holy Spirit, "power" has become much more accessible in the church. Wisdom, however, lags behind and the result is imbalance and disarray. The Spirit is now seeking to pour forth a wisdom we never dreamed possible. This outpouring could lead us into a new age of Jesus Christ! This is a badly needed, most important book, not only for the Charismatic Renewal, but for the whole church.

GRAINS OF WHEAT $3.50

Kelly B. Kelly. This little book of words received in prayer is filled with simple yet often profound leadings, exhortations and encouragement for daily living. Within the pages are insights to help one function as a Christian, day by day, minute by minute.

LIVING FLAME PRESS
Box 74, Locust Valley, N.Y. 11560

QUANTITY

_____	Becoming a Christian Person — 5.95
_____	Love in Action — 5.95
_____	Manna in the Desert — 5.95
_____	Reconciliation — 5.95
_____	Post-Charismatic Experience — 4.50
_____	Finding Peace in Pain — 3.50
_____	Thirsting for God in Scripture — 2.95
_____	Praying With Mary — 3.50
_____	Journey Into Contemplation — 3.95
_____	Spiritual Direction — 5.95
_____	Encountering the Lord in Daily Life — 4.50
_____	The Returning Sun — 2.50
_____	Bread for the Eating — 3.50
_____	Living Here and Hereafter — 2.95
_____	Praying With Scripture in the Holy Land — 3.95
_____	Discernment — 3.50
_____	Discovering Pathways to Prayer — 3.95
_____	Mourning: The Healing Journey — 2.95
_____	The Born-Again Catholic — 4.95
_____	Wisdom Instructs Her Children — 3.95
_____	Grains of Wheat — 3.50

NAME _____

ADDRESS _____

CITY _____ STATE _____ ZIP _____

Kindly include postage and handling on orders. $1.00 on orders up to $10; more than $10 but less than $50, add 10% of total; over $50, add 8% of total. Canadian residents add 20% exchange rate, plus postage and handling. N.Y. State residents add 7% tax unless exempt.